The distinctive logo of *LIFEPLANNING*, as it appears on the cover, is symbolic of a road. Throughout history, the road has been utilized metaphorically to describe the journey of life. Each and every one of us has come to that figurative "fork in the road" at least once, where the decision we make impacts the rest of our life.

LIFEPLANNING is a book about preparing for the best days of your life on Earth. The central message of *LIFEPLANNING*, though, is to begin preparing now, so that you will be ready when you reach the fork in the road.

LIFEPLANNING

A PRACTICAL
STEP-BY-STEP
GUIDE TO
PREPARING FOR
THE HAPPIEST
HEALTHIEST
AND WEALTHIEST
DAYS OF YOUR LIFE

BY ROBB E. DALTON

Published
By:
D.M. Wordsmith

The fundamental principles of this book are based on common sense and common knowledge. The information is shared in an effort to help the reader better prepare for the challenges of living. At no time is the author rendering medical, legal, financial, or professional advice. If assistance is sought in any of these areas, expert consultation should be obtained. The author and publisher specifically disclaim any liability, loss, or risk, personal or otherwise, of the use and application of any of the contents of this book.

ATTENTION: CORPORATIONS, CLUBS, AND SCHOOLS
LIFEPLANNING books are available at quantity discounts with bulk purchase for business, educational, and club use. For information on how to order write to:

LIFEPLANNING
P.O. Box 1490
Sun City, Arizona 85372

ACKNOWLEDGEMENTS

LIFEPLANNING is shared with the public both through this book and a comprehensive television community outreach campaign. The individuals and two consulting firms listed here each made contributions to the creation, production, or development of this project. In addition, I would like to thank the many professionals who gave generously of their time and expertise and the scores of volunteers who agreed to be interviewed or take the *LIFEPLANNING* tests.

EDITING	Dale Messmer	D.M. WORDSMITH
	Vicky Collins	KAKE TELEVISION
RESEARCH	Julie Griffith	DARTMOUTH UNIVERSITY
RESEARCH VERIFICATION	Lee Pioske	WORLD TRADING GROUP
GRAPHIC DESIGN & ILLUSTRATION	Judith Coast	JUDITH COAST GRAPHIC DESIGN
ADMINISTRATIVE	Amelia DiLella, Veronica Dalton, Mary Blair, Brad Gavigan	
MEDIA CONSULTATION	Darrell Ewalt	KAKELAND TV
	Jim Willi	KPNX TELEVISION
	Vicky Collins	KAKE TELEVISION
	Ron Loewen	KPLC TELEVISION
	John Marquiss	KTPX TELEVISION
	Quillen, Elsea, and Janzen, Inc.	
	Audience Research and Development	
PRINTING CONSULTATION	Kenneth Blair	

Special thanks to C. E. "Pep" Cooney
President & General Manager KPNX TV

*To my father, who in his life taught me the importance of living each day to its fullest, and who in his premature death taught me the importance of **LIFEPLANNING.***

TABLE OF CONTENTS

PART ONE

THE CHANGING WORLD
AND CHANGING YOU

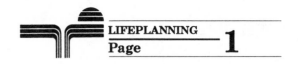

WARNING

"The life which is unexamined is not worth living."

Plato

Are you healthy? Happy? Wealthy? Loved? Are you comfortable with your career and its rewards? Do you enjoy hobbies and recreation that challenge you physically and mentally? Do you believe that your life is on the right track and going in the direction you desire? Do you have satisfying relationships on both friendly and intimate levels? Are you starting and ending each day with a positive feeling about life? ARE YOU WINNING?

If you answered "yes" to all the above questions and feel you are as healthy, wealthy, loved, challenged and fulfilled as your potential will allow, put this book down and start writing one.

If, on the other hand, you feel there is room for improvement in any of these key areas of living, welcome to *LIFEPLANNING*.

While most books begin with a preface or an introduction, this one starts with a warning. It is simple and straightforward: If you are not between the ages 21

to 65, equipped with a formal education, a satisfying career path, varied interests and satisfying relationships, this book was not written specifically for you.

While it is true that anyone can benefit from the information contained in this book, the reason for our warning is that this book has two specific goals targeted for a particular audience.

The first goal is to make this age group aware of the challenges they will face due to the aging of America. The second goal is to provide the necessary materials to assist readers in assessing their lives now and beginning an immediate self-improvement program.

At the same time, this book promises no magic potions or miracle cures. The truth is, if you do not enjoy a certain measure of success now, there is probably little this book can offer you. This is a book for people already on their way to the good life, people who are enjoying growth and success and wanting more.

It is my conviction that each and every one of us has the sole responsibility for our destiny. We have the power to improve our lives now, as well as to prepare for those important years of our life that follow our main career.

It is also my belief that if you cannot find the typical characteristics of happiness in your maturing, adult life, it is highly unlikely that you will achieve them in your latter years. Statistics also would indicate that without a modicum of success during your maturing life, you may not have the resources or health to enjoy those latter years.

On the following pages, all the elements of living - health, wealth, recreation, career, and companionship - will be discussed in depth. It's a book you read with a pencil - many chapters include participatory tests that will help you project your individual needs and likely realizations based on your lifestyle today. During the 10 chapters, you will eliminate the guesswork of how you are doing in life's key areas, and then you will develop a personal action plan to improve those areas where you are falling short of your desires.

It should be noted that this is not a book on retirement. Rather, this is a book dedicated to helping you deal with today's challenges to ensure that no part of your life or your future is dull or unproductive.

Common sense and common knowledge are the fountainheads from which this book flows. Throughout, the approach is practical, thorough, and to the point. In anticipation of some of your questions, the most informed people available were consulted, and exhaustive research was done with business, economic, medical, census, and government publications and periodicals. In an

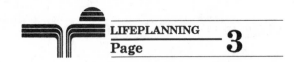

effort to better understand how people look upon their own successes and failures in life (the clarity of hindsight), hundreds of retired people were interviewed, and for a period of time, the author lived in one of the world's best known retirement communities.

As stated earlier, no magic potions or miracle cures came out of all the interviews, reading, and research. If anything, *LIFEPLANNING* reveals that the secret to preparing for success is no secret at all. Preparation for success during anytime in life is typically the end result of applying hard work, common sense, intelligence, and discipline to a well-defined set of goals.

LIFEPLANNING will prove invaluable in providing that set of goals. You must provide the hard work, common sense, intelligence, and discipline.

Now that we have defined our objectives, we can begin. Remember this book is your map for selecting the fork in the road that will turn your life into a healthy, happy, rewarding, and productive time. This is *LIFEPLANNING*.

Robb E. Dalton

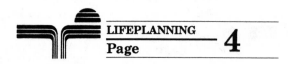

CHAPTER ONE

LIFEPLANNING:
THE FUTURE

I. THE FUTURE

"The winds and waves are always on the side of the ablest navigators."

Edward Gibson
"Decline and Fall of the Roman Empire"

The future that lies ahead for the people between the ages of 25 and 54 will be unlike any other time in the history of civilization. No segment of today's adult population represents a larger share of the total than those in this age group.

In large part, this group is made up of post-World War II offspring. They were born specifically between the years of 1946 and 1964, and are often referred to as the Baby Boom Generation.

Baby Bulge might be a more appropriate term. Today, one third of the total population was born between 1946 and 1964, and those between the ages of 25 and 54 represent a whopping 55 percent of the adult population.

These figures become even more significant as this group ages. In the year 2000, this group will range in age from 38 to 67, and just a few years later, our country will have almost as many adults over age 50 as under. By the year 2020, approximately one in every five adults will be over age 60. In this same year, it is projected that 60-year-olds will outnumber 18-year-olds for the first time in our history. Already, those over age 65 outnumber adults under 25. Contrast this with the fact that just 60 years ago the average life expectancy of U.S. citizens was only 54, and the significance of our aging population begins to take hold.

This dramatic aging of America creates some tough questions for those who will live through it. How will this vast segment of our population support itself? Where will people live? How will they spend this expanding life expectancy?

More importantly, how will you support, survive, and spend this important time of your life? If you are like most people, you have no answers to these questions. But by reading this book, you are at least asking, and asking is the first step toward discovering these important answers.

If, at this point, you are still not certain that preparing or planning for your future is important, then consider some specifics. U.S. Census figures indicate that currently a little more than 10 percent of our population is age 65 or older. Yet, the daily headlines document clearly that Social Security is incapable of covering basic living expenses for those dependent upon it.

On the average, current Social Security payments amount to less than $600 per month for a retiree age 65 who was an average wage-earner during his career. To further complicate matters, the monthly Social Security debt (along with Medicare) accounts for almost a third of the federal budget and more than 50 percent of domestic spending.

According to Peter Ferrara in his book, *Social Security: Prospects for Real Reform*, "Something must be done to reduce the benefits promised to today's young workers." The reality is that when the number of people over age 65 receiving Social Security jumps from about 10 percent of our population to more than 20 percent, the necessary Social Security tax rate for employees and employers could run in the unaffordable range of 20 percent, 30 percent, and higher. It is the classic no-win situation. If Social Security survives at all, it is highly unlikely that you could survive on its meager monthly allowance. Additionally, some politicians are proposing "means testing," in which Social Security would be available only to the needy. A status to avoid in life at all costs.

What about choosing the location where you will spend this special period of your life? If you think it is ridiculous now to think about where you might live in 10 to 30 years, then consider some housing cost projections for a popular retirement area, Phoenix, Arizona. Twenty years ago, a modest retirement home (a 1,600-square-foot home with two baths in a desirable neighborhood) in Phoenix sold for about $18,400, with a monthly house payment of about $130. According to the real estate company, *Better Homes and Gardens*, the same home today would sell for $82,000 and, with current financing, would have an average house payment of more than $700 per month. Assuming comparable rates of inflation 20 years from today, that same home could cost as much as $400,000 and have a monthly house payment well in excess of $3,000 per month.

If you are currently living in a home that is valued at approximately $150,000, and you desire a comparable home 20 years from now, you can expect your costs to more than double. Unless you want to settle for a trailer on the outskirts of town, a little advance planning is in order.

FUTURE STICKER SHOCK

Predicting the future rate of inflation is guesswork at best. Assuming a rate of inflation similar to past years, we will be paying in just 240 months the following prices:

Soda pop	$2.50 a can
Milk	$5 a gallon
Gasoline	$6 a gallon
Tuna	$7 a can
College tuition	$25,000 a year*
Automobile	$40,000 and up**
Home	$300,000 and up***

Room, board, tuition, and fees
**American-made sedan*
***Three bedroom, 1,600 sq. ft.*

What about companionship? Sure, you are a lovable person, but let's look at some statistical odds based on current census data.

The 1980 Census tells us that there are only about eight men for every 10 women between the ages of 65 and 74. For people 75 and older, the ratio is approximately one man to every two women. No matter how lovable you might be, finding companionship in the latter years, especially for women, will be challenging.

For those who find companionship, there is certainly no guarantee that they will hold on to it. According to a projection by the National Center for Health Statistics, about half of all marriages will end in divorce. Another statistical fact: a single woman who is over 30 and is well-educated has a significantly reduced chance of marrying.

ARE YOU READY FOR THE FUTURE?

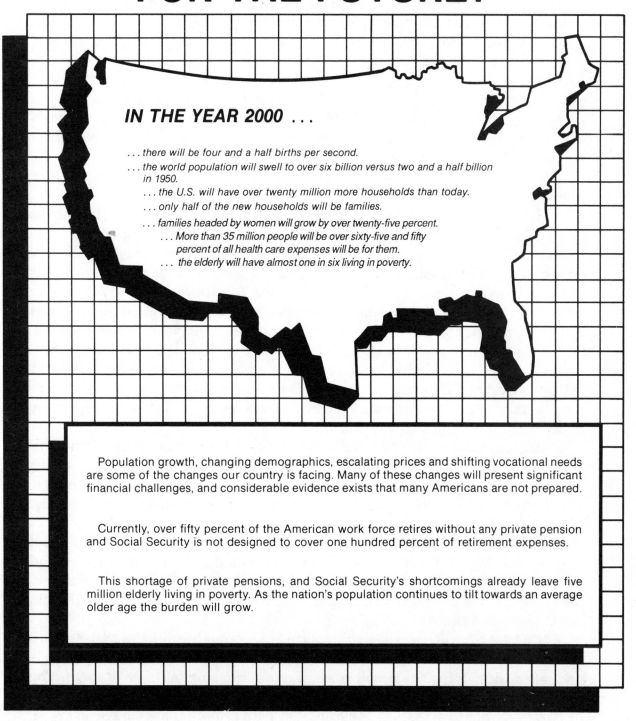

IN THE YEAR 2000 ...

... there will be four and a half births per second.

... the world population will swell to over six billion versus two and a half billion in 1950.

... the U.S. will have over twenty million more households than today.

... only half of the new households will be families.

... families headed by women will grow by over twenty-five percent.

... More than 35 million people will be over sixty-five and fifty percent of all health care expenses will be for them.

... the elderly will have almost one in six living in poverty.

Population growth, changing demographics, escalating prices and shifting vocational needs are some of the changes our country is facing. Many of these changes will present significant financial challenges, and considerable evidence exists that many Americans are not prepared.

Currently, over fifty percent of the American work force retires without any private pension and Social Security is not designed to cover one hundred percent of retirement expenses.

This shortage of private pensions, and Social Security's shortcomings already leave five million elderly living in poverty. As the nation's population continues to tilt towards an average older age the burden will grow.

This all adds up to staggering odds against this group of women finding success in marriage. Obviously, for every woman getting a divorce, there is also a man getting divorced, so no one escapes the challenge of finding meaningful companionship.

The Census Bureau also shares some startling facts on the statistics surrounding our children. For every 100 American children born today, only 40 will live in the traditional family environment. Another 40 will live in households split by divorce. Two more will live in households where a parent will die; and five will live with parents who will separate.

As you can see, companionship for everyone - young, middle-aged, old, single, married - will continue to be a challenge.

Switching to the important subject of health, many believe that the biggest cause of health-related problems in the years ahead will be lifestyle-related diseases. Already, modern medicine has all but eliminated the biggest killers of our ancestors. Diptheria, typhoid fever, measles, whooping cough, and small pox are all virtually wiped out in the United States. But they have been replaced in large part by medical problems of our own making. Cancer, strokes, heart attacks, cirrhosis of the liver, and diabetes now head the list of killers in America. Our smoking habits, alcohol consumption, diet, stress, and general lifestyle will play a big part in whether we face these problems in the future. Thomas Jefferson's admonition that we spend two hours a day taking care of ourselves now or two hours a day dealing with disease later in life seems especially appropriate advice in this day and age.

Jefferson's advice also seems compatible with *LIFEPLANNING*. The philosophy of *LIFEPLANNING* is that the best defense for the future is a strong offense today. The challenges presented by your aging, and the aging of America, will be many, and to more than survive, to in fact thrive in these times, we must anticipate, plan, and prepare.

LIFEPLANNING'S approach is to insist on success now. Each of us must analyze the key areas of our lives: health, wealth, recreation, career, and companionship. We must honestly and objectively assess how we are doing in these areas today. After an honest appraisal, we then need to set goals and begin working toward them.

LIFEPLANNING provides the tools to assess your life and the goals to work toward. You must provide honest answers to the *LIFEPLANNING* questions and, after identifying the problem areas, start working to improve them. The following chapters discuss in detail each of the key areas of living. These illustrations, along with the demographic growth projections you have just read, should be ample evidence that life 10, 20, and 30 years from now has the potential to be crowded, expensive, and unpleasant. But only if you fail to prepare.

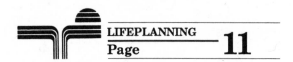
PART TWO

LIFEPLANNING:
THE PROCESS

II. HEALTH

"Shallow men believe in luck, believe in circumstances.
Strong men believe in cause and effect."

Ralph Waldo Emerson
"Conduct of Life"

Meet Michael. A typical American in many ways, he was many things to many people: father, husband, executive, friend.

Raised on a farm in the Midwest, Michael was working in a city. His life was similar to that of many men and women. He was married, the father of two sons, and a good provider. At age 42, he had worked his way up the ranks to the No. 2 position in an insurance agency.

He also had managed to work his weight up to more than 20 pounds above what it should be, his blood pres-

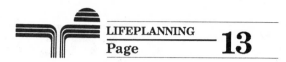

sure up to a dangerously high level, and his coffee drinking to several cups a day. He was well aware of the dangers of smoking, yet he continued. His idea of exercise was a round of golf in a motorized cart, a cooler full of beer always present.

Michael worked hard at his job, and his greatest pastime was daydreaming about owning his own business. He had owned several businesses earlier in life, and considered his dream-come-true to someday be his own boss again.

Michael's dream was to be short-lived. As he accumulated the expertise and capital necessary to once again own a business, he began experiencing shortness of breath, shoulder and chest pains, and in general, all the signs of a man whose heart was giving up on him.

It was the ultimate irony that when Michael finally reached a stage to begin a new life, life itself was running out.

In the early morning September 1, 1970, Michael M. "Mick" Dalton suffered a massive heart attack and died. Michael was my father.

My father's funeral was the first I had ever attended. Obviously, this experience left me, my teen-aged brother, and my mother devastated. The biggest tragedy, though, was that my father's death was premature and, in many ways, self-inflicted. His lack of meaningful exercise, his poor eating and drinking habits, his smoking, and his job-related stress took the greatest toll of all: his life.

He was, in too many ways, a typical American. As many Americans continue to neglect their health, they ultimately will pay that great price for their lack of self-care.

Heart disease is the No. 1 killer of adults in our country. Diet, driving habits, family medical history, personality type, and marital status also can add to or subtract from your quality of life and drastically affect your life expectancy. The medical community speaks with one voice on this subject: Many premature deaths could be delayed or eliminated if we would make significant lifestyle

THE RISE OF LIFE EXPECTANCY

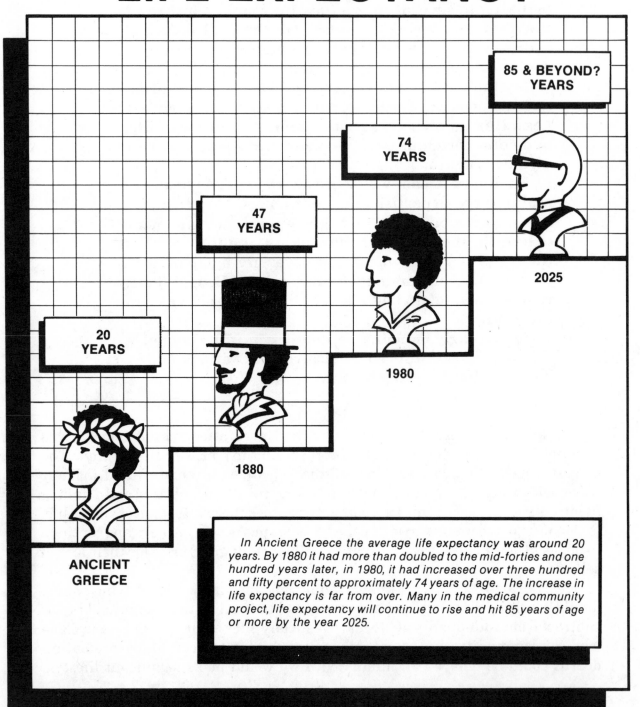

85 & BEYOND? YEARS

74 YEARS

47 YEARS

20 YEARS

2025

1980

1880

ANCIENT GREECE

In Ancient Greece the average life expectancy was around 20 years. By 1880 it had more than doubled to the mid-forties and one hundred years later, in 1980, it had increased over three hundred and fifty percent to approximately 74 years of age. The increase in life expectancy is far from over. Many in the medical community project, life expectancy will continue to rise and hit 85 years of age or more by the year 2025.

changes. By becoming familiar with the principles of good health and by applying them, we are almost certain to enjoy a longer and healthier life.

In ancient Greece, the average person could expect to live about 20 years. By 1880, human life expectancy had more than doubled, and 100 years later, in 1980, it had increased more than 350 percent, to about 74 years of age.

This rise is far from finished. Many in the medical community project that life expectancy will hit 85 years of age by the year 2025. Dr. Roy Walford, noted professor of pathology at UCLA, believes that someday it may be possible to live 130 years.

The dramatic increase in life expectancy during the 100 years between 1880 and 1980 was due primarily to the elimination or dramatic reduction of infec-tious diseases. (The one notable mortality statistic that has in-creased during this same period is acci-dental death, largely attributable to the automobile.) Better nutrition and better infant care also were contributing factors.

> ## THE SEVEN WARNING SIGNS OF CANCER
> Watch for these warning signals. If you have a warning sign, see your doctor.
> - A change in bowel or bladder habits.
> - A sore that does not heal.
> - Unusual bleeding or discharge.
> - Thickening or lump in breast or elsewhere.
> - Indigestion or difficulty in swallowing.
> - Obvious change in mole or wart.
> - Nagging cough or hoarseness.
>
> *Source: American Cancer Society*

While some as-pects of aging, such as gray hair or loss of elasticity, cannot be modified, other variables that determine how long you will live are very much in your control. Many experts believe that better nutrition, regular exercise, and lifestyle modification are the keys to continued increases in life expectancy. Dr. Art Mollen, a nationally respected nutrition and fitness expert and author of *The Mollen Method*, predicts that "the medicine of the 21st Century will be practiced only in part by the physician and mostly by the individual." People, Mollen writes, will be largely responsible for their health through proper nutrition and lifestyle, and physicians will play an ever-decreasing role in maintaining our health.

My father was becoming aware that he could have a tremendous impact on his odds of living a long, healthy life. But he was too late to make the necessary changes. His death robbed him not only of his life but of the opportunity to see his teen-aged sons grow into men, to see his wife become a successful executive in her own right, and to enjoy the birth of his beautiful grandchildren.

AIDS

Acquired Immune Deficiency Syndrome first hit the American medical scene in the early 1980s. Its discovery failed to make the front page news or attract significant attention primarily because it was a disease closely associated with homosexuality or heavy drug use.

Recently, all that has changed. Television newscasts and newspapers play AIDS stories prominently on a daily basis, telling us that we have an epidemic on our hands, and Americans are acutely aware that heterosexuals are at risk from the deadly virus.

While the numbers surrounding AIDS keep changing, the Center for Disease Control in Atlanta, has estimated that 1.5 million Americans are infected. Additionally, the Center projects that AIDS will be the second-leading cause of premature death, after accidents, among young men in America by 1991.

The three ways AIDS can be transmitted:
- Blood transfusions
- Sexual intercourse
- Needles and syringes

For more information, call
THE NATIONAL AIDS HOTLINE
1-800-342-2437

BLOOD PRESSURE

High blood pressure afflicts more than 50 million Americans and is the single biggest risk factor for stroke. Additionally, high blood pressure is usually without symptoms.

If you are diagnosed as having elevated blood pressure, follow these rules established by the American Heart Association:

1. Know your blood pressure.
2. Keep your weight at the proper level.
3. Do not use excessive salt.
4. Do not smoke.
5. Eat a low-fat diet.
6. Get regular medical checkups.
7. Take medication as prescribed.
8. Exercise regularly (under a doctor's guidance).
9. Live a normal life.
10. Encourage family members to have blood pressure checks.

If you are unsure about your blood pressure, get it CHECKED!

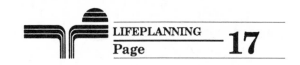

To help you live your fair share, please answer honestly the following questions in the test, "Will You Live Your Fair Share?"

WILL YOU LIVE YOUR FAIR SHARE?

The instructions for this first of five *LIFEPLANNING* tests are simple. Begin with the number 150 and add or subtract points after answering honestly each of the following questions.

Start the test with a score of   150

YOU

1. Do you have a managerial position that involves directing, disciplining, or reviewing multiple staff members? If yes, subtract four points.   -_____

2. Did you graduate from college? If yes, add two points.   +_____

3. Are you a type A personality (intense, aggressive, express feelings)? If yes, subtract six points.   -_____

4. Are you a type B personality (relaxed, non-aggressive, passive)? If yes, add six points.   +_____

YOUR FAMILY AND FRIENDS

5. If any two grandparents lived to age 82, add four points.   +_____

6. If anyone in your immediate family has (or had) cancer, a heart condition, or diabetes, subtract six points.   -_____

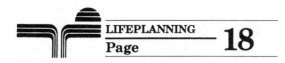

7. If anyone in your immediate family died from one of the above conditions, subtract an additional two points.

-_____

8. Are you married? If yes, add eight points.

+_____

9. Single and under 40? If yes, subtract two points.

-_____

10. Single and over 40? If yes, subtract four points.

-_____

11. If you live in a city, subtract four points.

-_____

12. If you live in a small town (less than 10,000) or rural area, add two points.

+_____

13. If you work in an office job, subtract four points.

-_____

YOUR LIFESTYLE

14. Do you smoke? If yes and 40 or more cigarettes a day, subtract 16 points.

-_____

20 to 40 cigarettes a day, subtract 12 points.

-_____

10 to 20 cigarettes a day, subtract six points.

-_____

15. Do you drink? If yes and more than 12 drinks per week, subtract two points.

-_____

More than 18 drinks per week, subtract six points.

-_____

16. Do you sleep more than nine hours a day?
If yes, subtract six points.

-_____

17. Do you have regular medical checkups? If yes,
add one point. If no, subtract two points.

+/-_____

18. Do you know your blood pressure and
cholesterol levels? If no, subtract one point.

-_____

19. Do you participate in strenuous exercise at least
three times per week for a minimum duration of 20
minutes? If yes, add six points.

+_____

20. Do you obey driving laws and wear a seat belt
whenever you are in a car? If no, subtract one point.

-_____

21. Do you take a vacation once a year? If no,
subtract two points.

-_____

22. Find your ideal weight according to the height
and frame size on the following chart. For every
four pounds you are over or under your ideal
weight range, subtract one point.

-_____

IDEAL HEIGHT/WEIGHT RANGE

HEIGHT (WITHOUT SHOES)				WEIGHT (WITHOUT CLOTHING)			
Men	**Small**	**Medium**	**Large**	**Women**	**Small**	**Medium**	**Large**
5'-1"	123-129	126-136	133-145	4'-9"	99-108	106-118	115-128
5'-2"	125-131	128-138	135-148	4'-10"	100-110	108-120	117-131
5'-3"	127-133	130-140	137-151	4'-11"	101-112	110-123	119-134
5'-4"	129-135	132-143	139-155	5'-0"	103-115	112-126	122-137
5'-5"	131-137	134-146	141-159	5'-1"	105-118	115-129	125-140
5'-6"	133-140	137-149	144-163	5'-2"	108-121	118-132	128-144
5'-7"	135-143	140-152	147-167	5'-3"	111-124	121-135	131-148
5'-8"	137-146	143-155	150-171	5'-4"	114-127	124-138	134-152
5'-9"	139-149	146-158	153-175	5'-5"	117-130	127-141	137-156
5'-10"	141-152	149-161	156-179	5'-6"	120-133	130-144	140-160
5'-11"	144-155	152-165	159-183	5'-7"	123-136	133-147	143-164
6'-0"	147-159	155-169	163-187	5'-8"	126-139	136-150	146-167
6'-1"	150-163	159-173	167-192	5'-9"	129-142	139-153	149-170
6'-2"	153-167	162-177	171-197	5'-10"	132-145	142-156	152-173
6'-3"	157-171	166-182	176-202	5'-11"	135-148	145-159	155-176

Source: Metropolitan Life Insurance Co.

QUESTIONS 1-22 TOTAL POINTS _____

YOUR OUTLOOK

This section of questions is important for rating your outlook on life, but <u>should not be included</u> in the total of questions 1-22 for determining your life expectancy. To answer these questions honestly, read them and answer immediately without hesitation and without saying what you think others want to hear.

23. Are you happy?   Yes   No

24. Do you have close friendships?   Yes   No

25. Are you satisfied with your work?   Yes   No

26. Are you generally satisfied with
your sexual activity?   Yes   No

27. Do you feel good about your future?   Yes   No

For each Yes answer, give yourself one point for a
maximum total of five points for this section.   +_____
Add your above score to your score from
 questions 1-22.

+_____

LIFETIME HEALTH SCORE   =_____

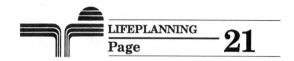

HOW TO INTERPRET YOUR SCORE

Your total score is important to record and save because it will be included in your overall **LIFEPLANNING** total and will help you in analyzing your status in the key areas of living. More will be said on this subject in Chapter Eight, The Balance. For now, you should know that a total score of less than 150 in questions 1-22 is potentially cheating you of valuable years of life.

While no test can predict exactly how long you will live, this test is based on the statistical data that in general denotes the major components of life expectancy. If you are losing points on the test through a habit or lifestyle pattern, you are playing a type of Russian Roulette.

HOW TO DETERMINE YOUR LIFE EXPECTANCY

To better illustrate how you might be shortchanging yourself, let's apply your test score to your own life expectancy. Remember that no test can determine your exact length of life, but so that we have something to go on, probability is calculated based on your answers and statistical averages for the nation. (It should be noted that dozens of variations on this style of test exist, and some debate continues on the life expectancy calculations.)

Now to convert your test score, first divide your total for Questions 1 through 22 in half.

(Your test score) divided by 2   =_____

Then make the following adjustments:

      Women 25 to 45 add 3 years   +_____

      Women 45 to 65 add 4 years   +_____

      Men 25 to 45 subtract 2 years   -_____

      Men 45 to 65, no adjustment   -_____

You now have an idea of how long you might live and what the problem areas are that might shorten your life.

The next section of this chapter contains the *LIFEPLANNING* 10 Commandments of Good Health, to help you specifically address problem areas and lengthen your life. Living according to these common-sense and common-knowledge rules of nutrition, exercise, and lifestyle can add valuable years to your life, as well as dramatically improve the quality of your life. The final section of this chapter, the *LIFEPLANNING* Library, contains recommended reading to further assist you in improving health and life expectancy.

If you are not serious about this important section of the book and what it tells you about your health, there is little reason to continue through the remaining chapters. If, on the other hand, you are encouraged by what you have learned about life expectancy and how you can dramatically influence it, then please continue because you are truly off on the right foot in your journey towards *LIFEPLANNING*.

LIFEPLANNING 10 COMMANDMENTS FOR GOOD HEALTH

In this chapter you have had an opportunity to find out what is wrong with your approach to health. Now you get a chance to set it right with these 10 commandments. Little argument will be found from the medical community on the importance of these general health guidelines. Each has been tested by time and the close scrutiny of the medical community. Overwhelming evidence establishes the importance of each of these rules, and your commitment to follow them could potentially add years to your life.

As always, individual health problems may make particular commandments unsuitable for you. If any question exists, or if you suffer from health problems, follow the 10 commandments of good health only after receiving the permission of your physician.

Finally, if the commandments seem as if they might be too time-consuming, think again. Rarely do good health habits take any more time than bad ones, and ultimately good health habits will give you more life to enjoy.

1. THOU SHALL NOT SMOKE

Even if you had been living in a cave for the last 15 years, it would be hard to escape all the warnings about the harmful effects of smoking. Simply stated,

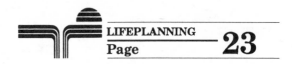

if you smoke, the most important move you can make for your health is to stop. Statistics point out if our nation could eliminate the No. 1 killer, heart disease, life expectancy could be increased approximately seven years.

In comparison, a 40-cigarette-a-day smoker could expect his life on average to be cut short by eight years. The damaging tars, nicotines, and carbon monoxides from smoking can cause considerable damage to the heart, lungs, teeth, tongue, throat, bladder, pancreas, esophagus, and blood. Lung cancer is caused in eight out of 10 cases by smoking, and annually more than 350,000 deaths are attributed to this dangerous habit.

Since the significant dangers of smoking are well-documented and well-known, it is probable that if you smoke, you have already tried to quit. If it did not work, do not despair. Hundreds of thousands of smokers have successfully quit and added years to their life. If you are ready to quit but need help, contact your physician, the American Lung Association, or a reputable treatment center.

If you are not ready to quit, understand that you literally trade years of life in exchange for the dubious pleasure of smoking.

II. THOU SHALL EAT A WELL-BALANCED, LOW-FAT, HIGH-FIBER, NUTRITIONAL DIET

In general, a person should eat three meals each day that are made up of a balance of the four food groups. Additionally, decreasing salt, fat, eggs, caffeine, sugar, red meat, junk foods, and sweets is sound nutritional advice. Increasing consumption of vegetables, fruits, and foods high in fiber, as well as switching to low-fat dairy products, are important elements of any sound diet.

An excellent set of dietary guidelines published by the Department of Agriculture and the Department of Health and Human Services advises cutting back on processed meats and cheeses and replacing them with fish, fowl, and low-fat dairy products. Increasing whole grains, fruits, vegetables, and staying away from highly processed (junk) foods, is also recommended. Developing sound eating habits is a matter of researching the basic guidelines developed by reputable organizations and implementing them.

The next and most important step is adhering to these guidelines as though your life depends on it - because it does. According to Walter C. Willet, M.D., a Howard University epidemiologist, "Diet is probably second only to cigarette smoking as a determinant of cancer in the United States."

Advice for developing a personal nutrition program fills many books. For more complete information, read the books on this subject recommended in the **LIFEPLANNING** Library and follow their advice.

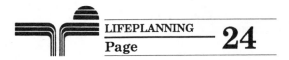

III. THOU SHALL DRINK SIX GLASSES OF WATER EACH DAY

Something as simple as drinking six glasses (minimum) of water each day is an important element of any personal health program. Drinking water reduces appetite, provides valuable nutrients, and keeps your skin's elasticity intact. Water consumption is also essential to keep the kidneys functioning properly, to assist circulation, and to rid the body of toxins. The price is also right. So bottoms up!

IV. THOU SHALL MAINTAIN THE PROPER WEIGHT FOR YOUR HEIGHT AND FRAME SIZE

Several medical studies on proper weight maintenance are at odds over the impact of being slightly overweight or underweight. No debate exists, though, on whether the extremes of obesity or malnutrition are dangerous. They are. Earlier in this chapter, you read the Metropolitan Insurance Company's recommended weight charts. To be on the safe side, your weight should fall within the published ranges of the weight standards for your height and frame size.

The National Institute of Health reports that "obesity is one of the greatest barriers of longevity." Overweight persons have an increased risk of dying from cardiovascular disease and have a tendency to develop hypertension and diabetes. Obesity also increases the chances of certain cancers by as much as 40 percent.

The sad fact is that many American adults over the age of 40 are overweight and the excess body fat is shortening their life expectancy.

Just as there is for smokers, a great deal of help is available in fighting the "battle of the bulge." The *LIFEPLANNING* Library includes excellent reading on this subject. Help is also available from many weight-loss clinics, and, as always, from your physician.

A final word on dieting is that fad diets rarely work over the long haul and are often based on poor nutritional advise. If the diet promises more than a pound or two in weight loss per month, the weight will probably return - your money will be gone forever.

V. THOU SHALL DRINK ALCOHOL IN MODERATION

To understand this good health rule, we first need to define moderation. Moderation for alcohol is no more than two ounces of alcohol per day. Since mixed drinks typically contain one ounce of alcohol, the limit for alcohol consumption

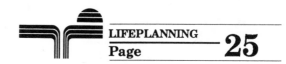

should be two mixed drinks per day or two glasses of wine or beer per day. In the excellent book on controlling stress, *Is It Worth Dying For*, doctors Robert Eliot and Dennis Breo cite medical evidence that drinking up to two ounces of alcohol per day also appears to increase the proportion of the so-called "good" cholesterol or high-density lipoprotein cholesterol (HDL). This type of cholesterol may help protect against coronary artery disease. Additionally, there is little argument that a couple of drinks after a long day can set a mood of relaxation.

This short list of positives associated with moderate alcohol consumption pales in contrast to the lengthy downside of drinking too much alcohol. Alcohol is a depressant that can aggravate an already sour mood or turn a good disposition into a bad one. Liver damage caused by excessive alcohol consumption is well-documented and, death because of cirrhosis of the liver has become a significant statistic. Depletion of Vitamin C, some of the B vitamins, and important minerals, coupled with alcohol's nutritionless calories, are additional reasons for keeping alcohol consumption to a minimum.

Several other, more technical reasons exist on why you should limit your drinking, but the bottom line is that the entire medical community speaks with one voice on the subject of alcohol. Do not drink at all or keep drinking at moderate levels. The rule on drug consumption is don't, unless under the supervision and prescription of a doctor.

VI. THOU SHALL ADHERE TO A SET ROUTINE OF AEROBIC EXERCISE

Aerobic exercises elevate your heart rate for prolonged periods of time and make the cardiovascular system provide additional oxygen. The body functions more efficiently and can better fight heart disease.

The additional benefits of aerobic exercise include better self-image, improved conditioning, and less stress. More and more research is linking aerobic exercise with increased longevity. In a study conducted by the Stanford University School of Medicine on almost 17,000 Harvard University alumni, researchers found that men who participated in a regular program of aerobic fitness had a lower rate of premature death than those who did not.

Walking, running, swimming, cycling, and aerobic dancing are all excellent aerobic exercises. Considerable information on developing an aerobic program is detailed in the *LIFEPLANNING* chapter "Recreation," but suffice to say that exercise should be as integral a part of your approach to good health as any other element.

VII. THOU SHALL TAKE A DAILY MULTIPLE VITAMIN CONTAINING THE RECOMMENDED DIETARY ALLOWANCES

Over and over again, it is stated that this book is based on common sense and common knowledge. Common knowledge tells us if we eat three meals a day that are nutritionally balanced, we will receive the necessary vitamins and minerals our body requires. Common sense tells us that, in a busy world, three balanced, nutritional meals from the four food groups are difficult to maintain.

Some debate continues as to whether vitamin supplements are necessary, and the medical community is slow to come out in complete support of this, but if you are not eating three balanced meals each and every day, a vitamin supplement is recommended. Since there is no data suggesting that a multiple vitamin containing the recommended dietary allowances is harmful, and there is much to suggest that too many of us are not eating three balanced meals each day, the prudent person will simply play it safe and smart.

Taking vitamins in amounts beyond the daily RDA should be done only with a physician's approval. Should problems arise, consult your doctor.

VIII. THOU SHALL REDUCE STRESS

Quite simply, stress **kills**. As stated on several occasions in this book, the No. 1 killer of Americans is heart disease. In the breakthrough book on stress, *Type A Behavior and Your Heart*, doctors Meyer Friedman and Ray H. Rosenman point out, "At least half the people who get heart attacks can be linked to <u>none</u> of the known and suspected causative factors - smoking, diet, exercise habits, other contributory diseases, and so forth." In their book, and in many other studies since, stress largely has been identified as the culprit responsible for many of these other heart attacks.

In *Is It Worth Dying For*, doctors Eliot and Breo go so far as to say, "In fact, stress may be the greatest single contributor to illness in the industrialized world."

In reducing stress, the first major obstacle is that stress and its effects on us are difficult to measure. In both of the above mentioned books, there are excellent tests and lists of common problems associated with stress. They will help you identify whether you are suffering from too much stress. In *Is It Worth Dying For*, the authors start the process of finding out whether you suffer from stress by asking, "Are you winning?" The book tells you, "If you answered no, chances are

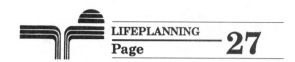

that you see yourself in a losing situation, without enough control over your life. You are a high-stress risk."

If you believe that stress is playing a negative part in your life, it is important to begin a program to calm it immediately. Many of the other *LIFEPLANNING* Commandments on Good Health, if followed, can help. Exercise, proper diet and weight control, stopping smoking, and keeping alcohol consumption at moderate levels are a great start. Avoiding high blood pressure, learning relaxation exercises, minimizing caffeine intake, and maintaining a positive self-image also are important ingredients in the stress-reduction recipe.

Finally, consulting with your physician and reading the above listed books will prove most helpful in stress reduction.

IX. THOU SHALL HAVE REGULAR MEDICAL AND DENTAL CHECKUPS

Too many Americans take better care of their car than their health. It is not unusual for us to have our car checked and serviced twice each year. Yet we wait until our health is in trouble before seeking the help of a physician. The problem with this approach is obvious. We can trade in our cars every year or so, but our bodies have to last us a lifetime. Without regular medical checkups, that life can be prematurely cut short.

The general rule of thumb for physicals is every three years for men under 40, every other year for men over 40, and annually for men over 60. Women of all ages should have gynecological exams, pap smears, and breast examinations every 12 to 18 months, depending upon the specific test and their physicians' advice. Significant family health problems or a history of personal illness should prompt individuals to adjust their timetable for medical checkups. As always, talk to your doctor about your own checkup timetable.

In four major health studies, including doctors from the American Cancer Society, the bottom line on checkups was that "all concluded that the frequency and content of checkups should be tailored to an individual's age, sex, and medical history."

Dental checkups are another important part of a health regimen that should not be ignored. They should be scheduled every six months and include thorough cleaning.

Finally, each of us should take the time to find a good physician and dentist. You should work to develop and maintain a solid patient/doctor relationship. Health care cannot be treated in an assembly-line fashion, and if your doctor fails to pay attention to you and have a firm grasp and interest in your medical history, find a doctor who will.

As Dr. Mollen tells us, health is becoming more and more a personal responsibility. If you know your astrological sign but not your own blood type, get smart and develop a doctor/patient relationship and an understanding of your own health. Remember, good health begins at home.

X. THOU SHALL REDUCE
YOUR VULNERABILITY TO ACCIDENTS

Rarely do we see any references to avoiding accidents in a list of tips on how to stay healthy. This seems odd when you consider that accidental death is always listed among the top 10 causes of mortality. While the medical and scientific communities have done a wonderful job reducing or eliminating infectious disease, accidental death has continued to climb. It is so serious a killer that it is now responsible for almost one half of all deaths among males between the ages of 15 and 50.

Earlier in this chapter, we said if we could give you only one piece of medical advice for your overall health it would be to stop smoking if you do smoke. On the subject of accidental death, if we were limited to only one piece of advice, it would be: Do not drink and drive. Alcohol and automobiles do not mix, and alcohol-related automobile accidents and deaths are the No. 1 cause of accidental deaths.

Observing driving laws, driving defensively, and wearing a seat belt also will go a long way in reducing your chances of being in a accident and will improve your chances of surviving one.

Another category with significant accidental death and injury is job-related. Because of the vast array of jobs and hazards unique to them, it is best to pay close attention to the rules and guidelines posted at your place of employment.

Finally, at the risk of sounding like a broken record, the other **LIFEPLAN-NING** Commandments on Good Health will help make you less prone to accidents. Smoking, obesity, stress, and the other health-related problems listed earlier can contribute to accidents.

LIFEPLANNING LIBRARY HEALTH

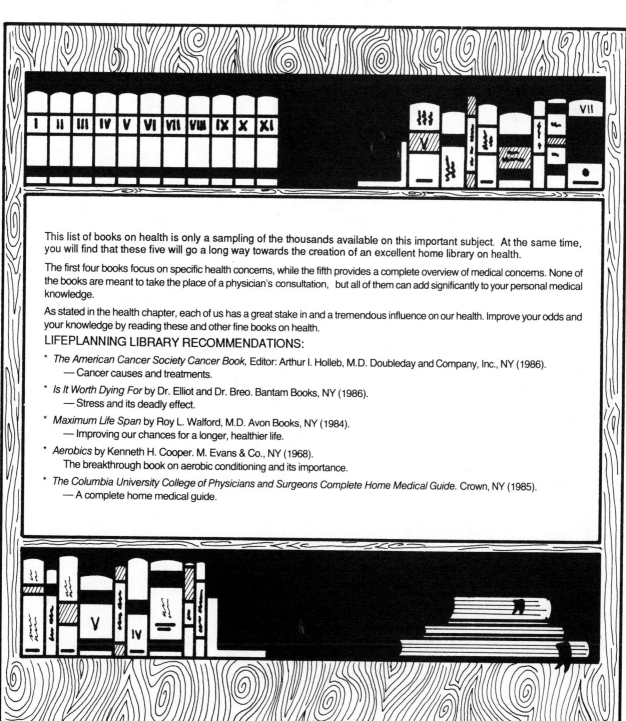

This list of books on health is only a sampling of the thousands available on this important subject. At the same time, you will find that these five will go a long way towards the creation of an excellent home library on health.

The first four books focus on specific health concerns, while the fifth provides a complete overview of medical concerns. None of the books are meant to take the place of a physician's consultation, but all of them can add significantly to your personal medical knowledge.

As stated in the health chapter, each of us has a great stake in and a tremendous influence on our health. Improve your odds and your knowledge by reading these and other fine books on health.

LIFEPLANNING LIBRARY RECOMMENDATIONS:

* *The American Cancer Society Cancer Book,* Editor: Arthur I. Holleb, M.D. Doubleday and Company, Inc., NY (1986).
    — Cancer causes and treatments.

* *Is It Worth Dying For* by Dr. Elliot and Dr. Breo. Bantam Books, NY (1986).
    — Stress and its deadly effect.

* *Maximum Life Span* by Roy L. Walford, M.D. Avon Books, NY (1984).
    — Improving our chances for a longer, healthier life.

* *Aerobics* by Kenneth H. Cooper. M. Evans & Co., NY (1968).
    The breakthrough book on aerobic conditioning and its importance.

* *The Columbia University College of Physicians and Surgeons Complete Home Medical Guide.* Crown, NY (1985).
    — A complete home medical guide.

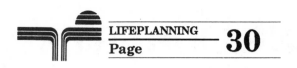

CHAPTER THREE

LIFEPLANNING: WEALTH

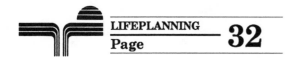

III. WEALTH

"Certainly, there are lots of things in life that money won't buy, but it's very funny - have you ever tried to buy them without money?"

Ogden Nash
"The Face is Familiar"

Meet David and Carolyn. In many ways, they are the typical upscale American couple. David teaches at the university, where he has the double pleasure of enjoying his work and earning a respectable income. Carolyn keeps busy raising their son, selling real estate part-time, and working on a variety of volunteer projects. They feel comfortable with their income and with their investments. They own their home and contribute the maximum amount each year to their IRAs. They thought their future was safe and secure.

David and Carolyn's security was short-lived because they were not prepared for the unexpected.

First, there was Carolyn's surgery. The medical expense that was not covered by David's insurance program through the university was small, but significant, and the post-operative care and prescriptions were costly. Additionally, Carolyn's pay completely depended upon commissions, and her inability to get out and sell real estate meant no income. Then, their son needed braces, and David's insurance did not cover dental expenses.

The downturn in oil prices provided the final pinch to their budget because of their heavy reliance on oil-based investments. Without Carolyn's income, they could not pay her monthly credit card and charge accounts, which all were at the limit. Perhaps the biggest surprise of all was that David was not aware of Carolyn's charge accounts, and Carolyn did not realize their investments were so heavily dependent upon oil.

In the case of David and Carolyn, we have both the exception and the rule. First, the two are to be commended for their earning power and retirement planning. As a rule, they would have been fine with their finances. The exception, of course, was their run of bad luck. While illness is not so unusual, their son's dental needs and their investment downturn were unanticipated. David and Carolyn's luck had run out.

The lessons to learn from studying David and Carolyn are many and important. First, the positive message is to earn a good living and put money away for retirement. Second, yet just as important, is to anticipate the unexpected in your planning.

In David and Carolyn's case, and for that matter everyone else's, insurance coverage for every medical contingency is a must. A coverage gap in health, life, homeowners, or automobile insurance can quickly turn your

WHERE MONEY GOES
The average American wage-earner works each year for:
4 months to pay taxes
10 weeks for housing
7 weeks for food
3 weeks for clothes
3 weeks for transportation
3 weeks for medical care
2 weeks for recreation
6 weeks for everything else

Source: Estimates Tax Foundation

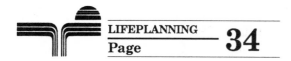

financial planning into a house of cards.

Their lack of a budget, Carolyn's charge accounts (mostly at 18 or 21 percent interest) taken to the limit, and their lack of investment diversification were some of their big financial pitfalls. Yet the biggest red flag was not knowing everything about their respective expenses and investments. This lack of knowledge and their bad luck placed them in the classic cash-flow crunch.

David and Carolyn are bright, capable people and will in time work their way out of their financial problems.

If you plan your finances properly, keep an eye out for financial red flags, and live according to the *LIFEPLANNING* 10 Commandments for Financial Wellness, you can greatly enhance your ability to avoid financial troubles.

The importance of money in each of our lives varies, depending on the person, but a national survey by *MONEY* magazine, "Americans and their Money 1986," reveals how we feel about it as a nation.

The survey found that money is the leading cause of family arguments. We borrow in record amounts to live in the style we have grown accustomed to, and one in every three people is convinced their sex lives would get better if their bank accounts were bigger. Almost one half of the people surveyed were unhappy with their finances, and more than 70 percent of Americans are in debt to the tune of $40,000, mostly from consumer borrowing.

In a poll conducted by *USA Today*, it was obvious that finances are a top priority among college students, too. Business majors almost double the next largest group, engineering majors. When students were asked to list the most important aspect of their lives that they want to differ from the lives their parents lived, the resounding answer was, "Better off financially."

Yes, money is important to us, and planning for life's financial aspects is essential. Once a person becomes responsible for his or her own finances, the planning cannot start soon enough.

A good place to start is with the age you have in mind when you think about your retirement. If you think that you will never quit working, then you need to ensure that working until you die is an option.

True, because of federal legistation the mandatory retirement age has been for all practical purposes negated. It also is likely that having fewer young people in the work force in the years ahead will provide new opportunities for those past age 65.

Even in light of these developments, nothing in your planning should be taken

HOW AMERICANS SPEND THEIR MONEY

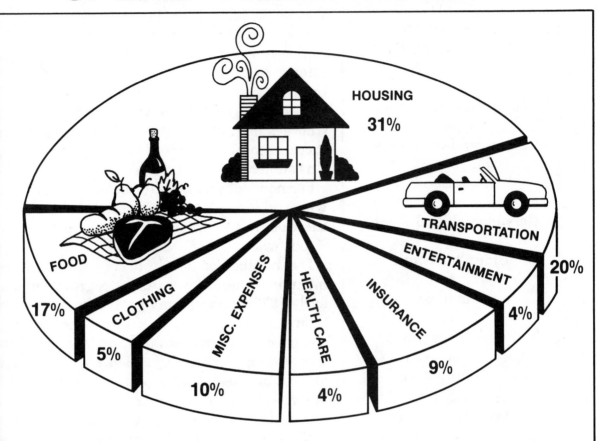

HOUSING 31%

TRANSPORTATION 20%

FOOD 17%

CLOTHING 5%

MISC. EXPENSES 10%

HEALTH CARE 4%

INSURANCE 9%

ENTERTAINMENT 4%

NATIONAL AVERAGES*	IDEAL RANGE	YOUR EXPENSES
31% Housing	25 - 29% Housing	_____ Housing
20% Transportation	13 - 16% Transportation	_____ Transportation
17% Food	14 - 18% Food	_____ Food
5% Clothing	3 - 5% Clothing	_____ Clothing
4% Health Care	3 - 5% Health Care	_____ Health Care
4% Entertainment	3 - 5% Entertainment	_____ Entertainment
2% Savings	8 - 10% Savings	_____ Savings

*SOURCE: American Demographics

THE CLIMB TO FINANCIAL FREEDOM

Art, Stamps, Collections
▲
Commodities/Futures
▲
Raw Land
▲
Commercial Real Estate
▲
Blue Chip Stock
▲
Annuities
▲
Pension Programs
▲
Life Insurance
▲
Home Ownership
▲
Savings Accounts

Traditionally, the higher the risk or speculation, the higher up the list (or later) the investment should be made.

As the investments on the ladder rise, so do the levels of risk and potential rewards.

for granted. If you sincerely believe you want to stay on the job past traditional retirement age, you should investigate how your industry or company has treated people in similar situations. More importantly, during the years between now and then, an employee should look for ways to make him or herself invaluable (there is no such thing as indispensable when it comes to filling a job). There will be more on this subject in Chapter Five.

For now, let's go back to the majority of you who will someday say, "enough is enough," those of you who will retire. The question is not if, but when.

The number of people taking early retirement in America continues to grow. In the early 1970s, approximately 20 percent of men between 55 and 64 took early retirement, compared to more than 30 percent today. If you want to stop working before age 65, you are not alone. The question is, at what age do you want to retire? Maybe a number instantly comes to mind. If so, hold that thought for a moment while we facilitate this process for everyone else.

In the preceding chapter, you had the opportunity to develop a reasonable expectation of how long you might live. Simple math will help you come up with the number of years you potentially have to enjoy once you pick a retirement age. Then, it is important to develop a financial plan to determine what those years of freedom will cost you.

To begin, a person must typically go through the following steps:

● Analyze and calculate your net worth. Find out your actual cash flow.

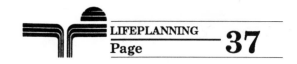

● Build an accurate budget .

● Determine your goals and objectives. Make a will.

Before you have finished reading this chapter, you will get a chance to do each of the above, or you will be pointed in the right direction to get the proper guidance needed to perform those steps.

Another goal before finishing this chapter is making up your mind to get and keep control of your financial future. By going through the above steps, taking the financial tests, and following the *LIFEPLANNING* commandments, you can better manage today's expenses and tomorrow's financial challenges.

Let's begin with a three-part test on your finances.

WILL YOUR MONEY RUN OUT BEFORE YOUR LIFE?

To take this financial wellness test, simply follow the instructions for the three sections and answer honestly all the questions.

Section One
YOUR FINANCIAL HABITS

This section is designed to find out if you have sound financial habits. Answer Yes or No to each of the following questions.

1. Do you have a properly prepared will, executed by an attorney, that you have reviewed in the last 24 months?   Yes   No

2. Do you have an IRA or KEOGH account that is contributed to annually?   Yes   No

3. Do you keep your credit cards paid up?   Yes   No

4. Do you know how much you owe?   Yes   No

5. Do you have a monthly budget, adhere to it, and keep it current?   Yes   No

6. Do you have adequate life, health, property, and automobile insurance? (see *LIFEPLANNING* Financial Commandment VI if you are unsure about what would be adequate coverage.)   Yes   No

7. Do you own a home? (to qualify for a yes, you must be in a home, making payments.)   Yes   No

8. Do you have more than a nodding acquaintance with your banker that allows you to reach him by phone and includes a degree of friendship/familiarity?   Yes   No

9. Do you have an acceptable credit rating?   Yes   No

10. Are you current on all monthly payments?   Yes   No

For each Yes answer, give yourself two points. If you have any questions on why these financial habits are important, read carefully the *LIFEPLANNING* Commandments for Financial Wellness at the end of this chapter.

RECORD AND SAVE YOUR SCORE   _____

Section Two
FINANCIAL KNOWLEDGE

This section is designed to see if you have a fundamental financial knowledge. Answer True or False to each of the questions.

1. The maximum amount an individual can contribute to an Individual Retirement Account is $2,000 annually.   True   False

2. The best place to keep a will is a safety deposit box.   True   False

3. A husband and wife should each have a will.   True   False

4. Social Security was designed to cover 100 percent of your cost of living during retirement.   True   False

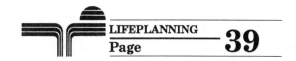

5. Ten percent of the population owns more than 70 percent of the nation's wealth.

True False

6. The best approach to family financial planning is traditionally to have the husband be the resident expert, and the wife focus on other areas.

True False

7. A KEOGH plan was designed for the self-employed to save for their retirement.

True False

8. Probate is necessary only when a will has not been executed.

True False

9. Whole life, ordinary, and straight life are identical forms of insurance.

True False

10. Alimony payments are not tax deductible.

True False

The even numbered questions are all false. The odd numbers are all true. Give yourself one point for each correct answer. Once again, if there are any questions you missed, read through the *LIFEPLANNING* Commandments for Financial Wellness at the end of this chapter.

RECORD AND SAVE YOUR SCORE _____

Section Three
FINANCIAL PROFILE

This section is designed to determine how you are actually handling your money.

1. Does your monthly home mortgage exceed
33 percent of your gross annual income?   Yes or No
    A. Total and enter all your monthly housing costs
    (mortgage, specials, insurance, and upkeep)   _____
    B. Multiply your monthly housing costs   x 12
    C. Your annual housing costs   = _____
    D. Write in your total annual gross
    income (wages, interest, dividends, rents,
    royalties)   _____
    E. Multiply your total annual gross income   x 33%
    F. Your annual housing limit   = _____

If line C exceeds line F, you are probably spending too much on your housing expenses and must answer Yes to question 1. There are always circumstances that can potentially change what your annual housing limit should be. Where you live and how you live can allow the limit to go up or down, but financial institutions generally use the 33-percent figure as the maximum allowable percentage of your housing costs, and you should too. If you limit monthly housing costs (line A) to principal and interest, your allowable percentage (line E) should be no higher than 28 percent.

2. Do you have less than two months take-home pay
in an emergency savings account?   Yes or No
    A. Monthly take-home pay   _____
    B. Multiplied by 2   x 2
    C. Your emergency reserve needs   = _____
    D. The amount you actually have in
    emergency savings   _____
If line D does not exceed line C, you must answer Yes to question 2 on emergency savings.

3. Does your monthly installment debt exceed
12 percent of your monthly take-home pay?   Yes or No

    A. Determine your monthly take-home pay   _____

    B. Multiply your monthly take-home pay
    by 12 percent   x   12%

    C. This is your maximum monthly installment
    debt .   =_____

    D. Total and enter all your monthly installment
    debt. (Installment debt includes auto, personal, and
    credit card payments - DO NOT INCLUDE
    MORTGAGE PAYMENTS)   _____

If line D exceeds line C, you must answer Yes to question 3 on installment
debt.   _____

4. Do you save less than 7 percent of your annual
income?   Yes or No

    A. Write in your annual income   _____

    B. Multiply by 7 percent   x   7%

    C. Your annual savings target   =_____

    D. Your actual annual savings contributions   _____

If line D is less than line C, you must answer Yes to question number 4.

5. Do you have less net worth than you should for
your annual income?   Yes or No

    A. Begin by writing in your total annual income   _____

    B. Multiply this amount by 4   x   4

    C. Your net worth target   =_____

    D. Enter in your net worth total (to help you
    determine your net worth, review the enclosed
    net worth worksheet)   _____

If line D is less than line C, you must answer Yes to question 5.

For each NO answer in the financial profile section, you receive 4 points.
      RECORD AND SAVE YOUR SCORE   _____

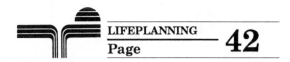
DETERMINING YOUR NET WORTH
Assets/Liabilities Worksheet

ASSETS	Current Market Value
Checking Accounts	_____
Savings Accounts	_____
Home	_____
Other Real Estate	_____
Life Insurance (Cash Value)	_____
Pension (Vested Cash Value)	_____
Automobiles	_____
Personal Property (Collections, Jewelry, Paintings, etc.)	_____
Business Interests	_____
Savings Bonds	_____
Time Deposits	_____
Other (Market Value)	+_____
TOTAL	=_____

LIABILITIES	Currently
Mortgage	_____
Automobile Loans	_____
Installment Loans	_____
Personal Loans	_____
Other (Taxes due, business debt, etc.)	_____
TOTAL	_____
TOTAL ASSETS	_____
TOTAL LIABILITIES	-_____
TOTAL NET WORTH	=_____

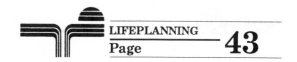

To figure your total score for the financial test, record your three scores and total:

Financial Habits Score   +_____

Financial Knowledge Score   +_____

Financial Profile Score   +_____

TOTAL FINANCIAL SCORE   =_____

HOW TO INTERPRET YOUR SCORE

Your total score is important to record and save because it will be included in your overall *LIFEPLANNING* total and will help you analyze your status in the key areas of living. More will be said on this subject in Chapter Eight, The Balance.

For now you should know that a total score of fewer than 40 points indicates a financial situation that needs some fixing. While no test can predict exactly how you should conduct your financial affairs, this test is based on sound personal financial guidelines.

If you are losing points in the financial habits section, you could be risking your credit rating and getting in over your head with debt. If you missed two or more questions on the financial knowledge section, you need to brush up on your financial reading and overall financial level of sophistication. Missing one or more questions on your financial profile means you are not accumulating assets and building your financial strength at an acceptable level.

The bottom line is that you should not settle for a score of less than 50 as you near age 50. Until age 40, you should work, save, budget, and invest to maintain a score at least 10 points higher than your age.

These general guidelines will go a long way toward ensuring a comfortable retirement. Do not despair if currently you are coming up short. The message is clear, and the problem areas are now identified. Let's now look at some ways to improve your overall financial wellness.

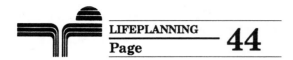
THE LIFEPLANNING 10 COMMANDMENTS FOR FINANCIAL WELLNESS

Financial common sense can vary from person to person according to earning power, number of dependents, current level of debt, and family financial elements, but in general, the financial community stands in support of the following guidelines.

These commandments might seem like a lofty set of goals. They are. Your finances are key to your complete enjoyment of life, and you must work hard and be smart to ensure success in this important area. Remember, only two percent of the population will retain their standard of living upon retirement, and almost one in every six of our citizens over 65 live below the poverty line. Our lifestyle today, as well as our financial future, is our responsibility. Let's make sure it is based on sound financial principles.

I. THOU SHALL HAVE A PROPERLY EXECUTED WILL

It is difficult to select the most important of all the financial principles, but certainly one of tremendous importance is this commandment.

A will is a legal document that sets forth the distribution of your assets upon your death. It is important to properly distribute your possessions to selected beneficiaries, to ensure that your wishes are carried out, and to eliminate any unnecessary expenses. Care for minor children and tax considerations are two additional and important reasons to draw up a will.

To ensure that your will is properly prepared, it is important to retain a reputable attorney. Both spouses should have their own wills and have them reviewed at least every other year or whenever they have experienced significant change in their life.

The final word on wills is that there are few legitimate reasons to avoid having one. Make an appointment to see your attorney today.

II. THOU SHALL DEVELOP A FRIENDLY, PROFESSIONAL RELATIONSHIP WITH A BANKER

Ironically, this is advice that is seldom given out, yet it is a key element in developing financial clout. The best way to begin this relationship is to consolidate all of your banking with one bank. Checking, savings, credit cards, IRAs, loans, special accounts, installment debt, safety-deposit boxes, and so on should be with one financial institution. Getting acquainted with a banker is a matter of arranging an introduction through a business colleague, friend, or by approaching the banker and introducing yourself.

Despite the claims made by bank advertising, unless you have unusual needs, banks, because of heavy regulation and competitive pressures, all offer services of a similar nature. While some minor differences such as checking charges or automatic bill-paying features exist, choosing a bank based on these options is short-sighted. Your ability to get to the banker and obtain a business loan, home mortgage, student, or automobile loan at excellent rates is far more important. Interest paid on investments and proper insurance for deposits are the other keys to selecting your bank.

This advice also carries over to other types of financial matters. Whether it is a stock brokerage, insurance agency, or savings and loan association, funneling your business to one company in each respective area elevates your status and enhances your negotiating position.

III. THOU SHALL BUY A HOME

Owning a home should be an important building block in your financial stability. The advantages are numerous:

- Home ownership builds equity that renting does not.
- Home ownership creates an automatic form of savings.
- Home ownership, under the new tax laws, provides a significant deduction of mortgage-interest payments.
- Under tax reform, home loans are one of the few tax-deductible loans left. A loan against your home equity can help finance traditional consumer purchases and keep the interest deductible. Consumer loan interest is being phased out, leaving non-home owners at a buying disadvantage.
- Home ownership is a hedge against inflation and an excellent method of accumulating a nest-egg for retirement.
- Home ownership is emotionally satisfying.

Buying a home is traditionally one of the largest purchases a person will make in a lifetime. Considerable care and research should be invested before buying or building a home.

Like diet and nutrition, all the advice necessary to making a wise home buying decision can and does fill many books. Information on several fine books covering this subject as well as other financial matters is listed at the end of this chapter in the *LIFEPLANNING* Library. Regardless of how you get the message, make sure it sinks in. Investigate the housing options and obligations available and see if owning a home makes financial sense for you.

IV. THOU SHALL MAINTAIN AN EXCELLENT CREDIT RATING

A credit rating is how you are viewed in terms of your bill-paying history, and establishes the total amount a lender will allow you to owe them. Getting credit in today's world is easy. To lose it, simple. To regain it, difficult.

All of us as children were chastised to be good or have a bad mark go on our "permanent record." As we grew up, we found out that, for the most part, those were empty threats. Risking your credit rating will go on your permanent record, and that is not an idle threat. It is a real problem that can prevent you from owning a home or an automobile, or from enjoying the convenience of paying on installment. The single most important way to protect your credit rating is to pay your bills on time.

Here are some signs of credit problems to watch for and avoid:
- Family arguments over money.
- Past-due notices or creditors calling.
- Credit lines on charge accounts and credit card purchases at the limit.
- No savings.
- Relying on cash advances or credit to meet monthly bills.
- Borrowing to pay bills.

V. THOU SHALL DEVELOP AND ADHERE TO A PERSONAL BUDGET

Let's be honest. Budgeting is like dieting. We know it is good for us, but we rarely stick to it. At the same time, with the right approach and a little perseverence, financial flab can be trimmed away and monetary muscle toned.

To develop a realistic budget, a person should go back over the last 12 months of credit-card charges, check stubs, and installment debt. As best as possible, a budget of what you spent during the past 12 months should be constructed.

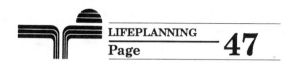

Amounts for each month for all the major expense categories should be developed. Food, housing, transportation, medical, business, recreation, insurance, education, and savings are the classic areas of expense.

After reviewing the past 12 months, build a budget for the next year, taking into consideration any projected changes. Several budget worksheets and guidelines are available through your financial institution, insurance agent, or in the books recommended in the *LIFEPLANNING* Library.

A general rule of thumb that can help you eliminate budget troubles is to keep your total after-tax income in the following ranges:

> HOUSING COSTS: 30 percent or below
> SAVINGS: 7 percent or higher
> CONSUMER DEBT (including transportation): below 15 percent
> CLOTHES/ENTERTAINMENT: below 10 percent
> MEDICAL EXPENSES: 5 percent

Keep your budget up-to-date and simple. Most importantly, stick to it. It requires a small investment of your time that pays off dividends in personal money management.

Finally, as the saying goes, "The only things in life that are certain are death and taxes." If you do not have a thought-out tax plan, your taxes will often be the death of your financial planning. Talk to your accountant or tax planner to forecast annual tax obligations so you are not surprised at tax time. The general rule of thumb is to pay enough during the year to avoid large tax bills or refunds. Additionally, a large swing in income will often alter your tax obligations.

VI. THOU SHALL HAVE ADEQUATE INSURANCE

Automobile, homeowners, hospitalization, mortgage, ordinary, property, term, and whole-life insurance are some of the many types of insurance available from a multitude of companies. "Do not buy," "raise the deductible," and "lower the deductible" are just some of the advice circulating concerning insurance buying.

The contradictory advice stems from the number of policies available. The best advice is to find an excellent insurance agent who will take the time to help you evaluate all your insurance needs and make sure your home, possessions, automobile, family, and life are adequately covered.

Some general insurance guidelines to follow are that your deductibles should

be no higher than you can afford to pay in case of loss; your liability/coverage limits should be the maximum available; and your life insurance coverage should allow a family to maintain its standard of living in the event of a death. Also, umbrella coverage can bring additional peace of mind and added protection at low rates.

Finally, some financial advisors suggest cutting back on insurance to save money. We submit that not having enough insurance can unnecessarily complicate an unpleasant loss. See several agents: shop, compare, and insure.

VII. THOU SHALL PLAN, PREPARE, AND SAVE FOR RETIREMENT

On several occasions in this book, we have taken great pains to point out the impact of the aging of America and our expanding life expectancy. Currently, about 30 percent of working men are taking early retirement, and this percentage continues to grow. It is not unusual for a person who retires early to have more than 20 years of living left after the paycheck stops.

According to the Bureau of Labor Statistics, the average retiree earning $40,000 annually can expect only 64 percent of his salary replaced by pension and Social Security dollars. What's more, more than 50 percent of today's work force is not covered by a private pension.

Serious questions certainly exist about the future of Social Security. In other words, unless you want a dramatic drop in your standard of living, you must have additional savings set aside for the future.

Several excellent alternatives exist in the form of IRAs, KEOGHs, and insurance plans. To encourage savings for retirement, the government has created several tax breaks for these types of plans. To get started, see your financial planner, stockbroker, insurance agent, or banker. Additional information on the many fine plans available can be found in the books in the *LIFEPLANNING* Library.

The years after your main career have the potential to be the most enjoyable or the most miserable of your life. Finances will play an important role in determining which it will be for you.

VIII. THOU SHALL DEVELOP A SAVINGS PLAN

No, this is not a repeat of Commandment VII. That savings advice is specifically for retirement and is important enough to warrant its own commandment. Many other facets of life also require adequate savings, such as education, vacations, special purchases, or a down payment on a home.

To determine your savings needs, analyze your life today and project what they will be in the future. If you have children, college costs should be accrued. If you and your spouse have always dreamed of a special vacation, a savings account is the best way to get started. Typically, each of these different areas of expense should have separate savings accounts. Depending on whether it is a short-term goal or a life-long ambition, you should visit with your financial advisor or banker to determine how to maximize your returns.

After setting your financial savings goals, a consistent way to ensure that your savings deposits are made is through payroll deduction. It is easy and painless.

Finally, a key fundamental of every savings program should be a special savings fund with a minimum of two months salary put aside in case of an emergency.

IX. THOU SHALL BE A COMPARISON SHOPPER

By consistently being thorough, attentive comparison shoppers, consumers can dramatically increase their buying clout. Too often in our busy, fast-paced world, we shop for convenience, and invariably cost ourselves hard-earned dollars.

Here are some sure-fire ways to stretch your shopping dollars:

● Avoid impulse-buying. This culprit has filled more closets with clothes worn once, cupboards with uneaten foods, and garages with dust-gathering junk than any half-price sale. Remember to shop before you spend.

● Hold down credit-card balances. The great bargains you find will turn out to be more expensive than the original retail price if you end up adding in 18-21 percent finance charges.

● Look around. You will be surprised to find that sometimes the same item can be sold for several prices in the same shopping mall. Before you ever leave your home, check the newspaper, the television, and circulars for sales. A little effort in comparing prices typically will result in significant savings. Look for the sales.

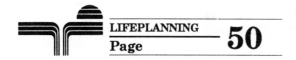
● Look for quality used merchandise. Garage sales and classified ads are two ways to save money on many items. They are also a good way to generate some extra shopping dollars. See what you have that is gathering dust and turn it into dollars.

Finally, the best money-saving tip on shopping might be to ask yourself a few questions: Why do you need this item? Did you need it six months ago? Will you need it six months from now? Will it appreciate or depreciate in value? Have you thought this purchase through carefully? Have you done your comparison shopping? By paying attention to your answers and going through the above exercises, you will be surprised what you can live without.

X. THOU SHALL NOT DEFINE THYSELF BY THY POSSESSIONS

"Keeping up with the Joneses " is a wonderful myth that more than 1,000 commercial messages bombard us with each and every day. Too often, we have fallen for the mistaken notion that owning a particular item will change our self-perception or how others perceive us. The truth is that material possessions rarely generate a lasting happiness. While it is certainly important to have nice things, it is just as important to not confuse the prestige or convenience those items provide with real happiness.

LIFEPLANNING LIBRARY WEALTH

As is the case with all the LIFEPLANNING LIBRARY suggestions, this list is a starter. Many books and other periodicals provide important financial advice and guidance. In fact, the books listed here recommend other excellent books you should consider. You should also visit with your banker and financial advisor for recommended financial reading.

The importance of personal finances should motivate all of us to read up on the subject. The four books listed here along with the magazine that is recommended will serve you well in matters of money.

LIFEPLANNING LIBRARY RECOMMENDATIONS:

* *Lifetime Financial Planning* by William E. Donoghue. Harper & Row, NY (1987).
    A financial strategy handbook with special attention on investing.

* *Ninety Days to Financial Fitness* by Don and Joan German. Macmillan Publishing Co., NY (1986).
    — Practical advice on how to fix-up poorly managed personal finances.

* *Creating Wealth* by Robert G. Allen. Simon & Schuster, NY (1983).
    — Advice on how to accumulate wealth with primary focus on real estate.

* *Sylvia Porter's New Money Book for the 80's* by Sylvia Porter. Doubleday and Company, NY (1979).
    — Complete home financial guide (Written in 1979).

* *Money Magazine*
    A no-nonsense magazine that teaches you through the examples of others how to deal with money.

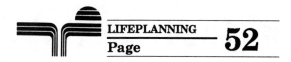

CHAPTER FOUR

LIFEPLANNING:
RECREATION

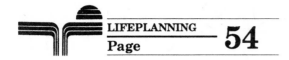

IV. RECREATION

"RECREATION: to create anew, restore, refresh . . . refreshment of strength and spirits after toil."

Webster's Dictionary

Meet Terry. As a child, she was agile, aggressive, and adept at every athletic endeavor she tried. She was a typical tomboy. At 29 years of age, she spent the minimum number of hours she could typing and performing administrative assistant duties for an electronics executive, and the balance of her time nurturing her passion for sports. She enjoyed aerobics before work, racquetball after. Softball in the summer. Skiing in the winter. Golf and tennis on the weekends. Ironically, with all of these activities that constantly put her in touch with others, she was still single, and in between the myriad of workouts, she felt her life was a little out of synch.

Meet Taylor, as delicate in appearance as she was deft with the touch of her violin. Taylor made music

her work, her pastime, her passion. She was second chair with the symphony. Since the second grade, she had been attached to her violin as if it were another limb. A total of 20 years. While she had a very clear career goal of ascending to first chair and ultimately moving to a larger symphony, the rest of her life was a bit murky. Like Terry, she had never married and, beyond playing the violin, all of life was little more than a necessary chore.

Meet Diana. Rarely was there time in her life for Terry's athletics or Taylor's music. Her life revolved around twin boys, age 3, and a 5-year-old daughter. From the moment she awoke in the morning until mid-evening, she was consumed with their care. The cycle was constant and never-ending. Each morning it began with getting the children up, washed, and fed. The balance of the day was spent tending to their crises and repeating the pattern of feeding and cleaning up after them. By the time the children were in bed each evening and the dishes and toys finally cleaned up and put away, it was all Diana could do to stay awake. As time went by, she had less and less in common with her husband when it came to conversations beyond the subject of the children.

Meet Lana. If Webster's Dictionary had a definition for "life of the party," her picture would be included. Already married and divorced at 25, her life revolved around a never-ending string of men. Exercise was a necessary evil to keep her figure attractive to her male companions. Music, concerts, and athletics all were the stuff dates were made of and of little real interest to Lana. The last book she had read was the driver's test manual when she went to renew her license two years ago. Her reading material came mostly from magazines. Her spare time, for the most part, was spent with different men.

Meet Alex. Systematic, orderly, and organized best described the world that Alex had created for himself. As an engineer, it seemed natural, but to the rest of the world, it made him the odd man out. Each of Alex's days consisted of nine hours of working and commuting, seven and a half hours sleeping, two hours watching the news and reading the newspaper, precisely 90 minutes eating his three meals, and one hour each day tending to the necessities of life, such as personal hygiene and paying bills. What little time was left over, Alex was glued to his personal computer.

As different as Terry, Taylor, Diana, Lana, and Alex are, they all have something very much in common. Their lives are out of balance. Throughout the pages of *LIFEPLANNING*, the importance of balance between the five key areas of life is emphasized over and over again. Health, wealth, recreation, career, and companionship in one's life are so interrelated that failure in one of these areas will make success all the more elusive in the other areas. Just as important, a true and lasting happiness is rarely found unless an individual can find symmetry within each of these key areas of living. Balance is necessary within each key area of living just as balance is essential between all the key areas.

While a good many pages could be devoted to why Terry, Taylor, and Alex turn their energies towards their personal projects instead of people or why Diana and Lana are getting lost in their relationships and neglecting meaningful recreation, these pages will instead focus on three more constructive tools for you. These tools should prove invaluable in helping you find your own personal symmetry in the area of recreation.

First, we will catalog some of the many outlets that are available to you in the area of recreation. Secondly, you will get the opportunity to assess how you are doing in this important area of your life. Finally, some excellent information is provided on how to begin, maintain, and improve your approach to recreation.

Whenever the term recreation is used in *LIFEPLANNING*, it will be defined

exactly as Webster defines it in the dictionary. Each of us probably gets a mental picture of an individual hobby, sport, or cultural activity that we enjoy when the term recreation is mentioned.

While that is fine, it is important you broaden your thinking of this word to Webster's definition: "to create anew, restore, refresh, refreshment of strength and spirits after toil: a means of refreshment or diversion." We want you to realize that Terry's life without cultural activities, Taylor's life without exercise and the tunnel vision of Diana, Lana, or Alex, are all dangerous. The danger is that you will not fulfill Webster's definition of "creating anew, restoring, or refreshing" your life with a complete approach to recreation.

A great deal of evidence points out that Americans, in general, are falling down in this important area. Several key statistics indicate a lack of recreational diversity, and in too many instances, a lack of recreation, period.

No better statistics point out this recreational deficiency than the constantly expanding time allotted by American households for television viewing. According to the Television Bureau of Advertising, television viewing has grown practically every year since its inception. Currently, the television is on for more than seven hours a day in the average American household.

Americans have become very adept at juggling a variety of tasks - like visiting, eating, doing homework, and talking on the telephone - with the TV on. But it is still almost incomprehensible for many people that one third of their total day, half of their nonsleeping day, and practically all of their free time is spent in the company of television.

In general, television is picked upon altogether too much and blamed for a variety of ills in society for which it can legitimately plead not guilty. Despite the unusual number of hours that American households have committed to daily television viewing, the television is not to blame but rather the viewer. People have used television as a babysitter, companion, and vicarious means of involvement in the world, when its purpose was never meant to be more than a medium for entertainment and information.

Watching the news and an additional two hours of entertainment viewing each day should more than adequately fulfill this purpose. As a rule, watching television in larger doses than this will only take valuable moments from our most precious commodity, our time.

Indiscriminate television viewing is just one of the abuses of our free time. The typical American watched many hours of sports last year on television, but rarely took part in an athletic activity. Additional evidence of America's sedentary lifestyle is obvious by the weight problems of more than 34 million Americans.

HOW AMERICA UNWINDS?

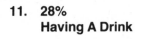

1. **62%**
   Watching TV

2. **60%**
   Doing Nothing

3. **56%**
   Vacationing

4. **55%**
   Listening To Music

5. **54%**
   Reading

6. **50%**
   Dining Out

7. **43%**
   Friends

8. **38%**
   Hobbies

9. **32%**
   Working Around The House

10. **31%**
    Sports/Exercise

11. **28%**
    Having A Drink

12. **25%**
    Movies

13. **18%**
    Cooking

14. **17%**
    Shopping

15. **13%**
    Having Hair Done

16. **1%**
    Sex

17. **1%**
    Religion

When a cross-section of American adults was asked how they like to unwind, the variety of answers was surprising, but not as surprising was the number one choice — watching TV. According to the Television Bureau of Advertising, TV viewing in the average American household is over seven hours per day.

Way down the list of how Americans like to spend their time are hobbies, exercise, movies and sex.

Source: D'Arcy, Masius, Benton & Bowles Survey

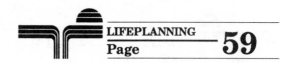

While physical inactivity is a real health and recreation shortcoming in our country, it pales in comparison to the great numbers of people who have turned away from important mental and cultural activities to enhance their free time.

Only half of the adult population has read a book in the last year that is unrelated to their work. The lion's share of concert, live theater, and museum attendance come from a tiny minority of the general public. Something as simple as a walk in the countryside has become a rarity.

The point of all this is simple. Americans in the last 30 years have allowed themselves to become more and more insulated from the world of first-hand experiences. Rather than participate in social, cultural, or sporting activities, we have become content to watch others. As we become more removed from the act of participation, we tend to place greater significance on the performance of others.

Our "peeping-Tom" mentality of watching others compete and participate has elevated those participants and performers to superstar status, with the lifestyles and wealth of royalty.

We watch these athletes or entertainers not only for the quality of their performance but with an eye on their lives off the playing field or stage. This idolatry gives the clothes they wear, the words they utter, and the lifestyle they lead special significance.

Our most-respected, most-admired lists consistently include the names of rock stars, quarterbacks, and actors instead of scientists, writers, and teachers. In turn, today's children get a distorted perspective of learning a musical or athletic skill and turn away from the art of learning these skills for the pure pleasure and enjoyment they bring.

WHAT AMERICANS ENJOY

On average, Americans attended, visited, read, or watched the following leisure activities in the last year:

Opera	3%
Ballet	4%
Jazz Performance	10%
Plays	12%
Classical Concert	13%
Musical Play	19%
Art Exhibit	22%
Read Novel or Poem	56%
Television	98%

Sources: A. C. Nielsen,
Bureau of Census, Performing Arts

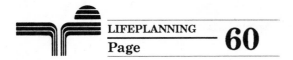

The point of all this is not that athletic or artistic excellence should not be recognized or rewarded. It should be, but as importantly, we must not replace our athletic or artistic attempts vicariously by watching others.

To facilitate the process of getting involved, here are three important areas of recreation. Each of us should have some level of involvement in several of the activities from each list. Additionally, a well-rounded, balanced person should be knowledgeable or proficient in at least one of the activities from each category.

ATHLETIC/SPORTING

walking	aerobics	soccer
swimming	handball	hockey
jogging	racquetball	bowling
cycling	weightlifting	skiing
tennis	softball	calisthenics
golf	basketball	sailing
dancing	baseball	scuba-diving
hiking	football	martial-arts

HOBBIES

collecting	card-playing	fishing
photography	camping	boating
music	gardening	sailing
painting	hunting	bird-watching
sewing	crafts	artwork
riding	billiards	hunting

INTELLECTUAL/CULTURAL

movies	reading	writing
museums	traveling	art galleries
concerts	thinking	performing arts

How did you do? Can you legitimately check off at least one item from each of the three categories? Are you actively involved and proficient in an athletic/

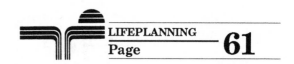

sporting endeavor? Do you have a regular hobby? Are you keeping your mind engaged with an intellectual or cultural pursuit?

If you think all these questions are silly and, of course, you and the rest of the world are actively involved in a variety of athletic and intellectual pastimes, you are wrong. According to a nationwide poll by the advertising agency D'Arcy, Masius, Benton, and Bowles, Americans confessed that watching television got the highest vote for ways to unwind, followed closely by "doing nothing."

Of course, this is not new. More than 25 years ago, President John F. Kennedy made himself clear on the subject of physical fitness when he challenged Americans to get off their duffs and fight the "growing softness of our country". If there is any chance that you are growing soft, it is time to do something about it.

The good news is that help has never been more abundant. The business of catering to those of you interested in getting started on the road to athletic, social, and intellectual fitness is filled with health clubs, community theaters, great books, friendly organizations, and instructors by the dozens.

The other important piece of information (and good news) that goes along with intellectual and athletic fitness is the wonderful knowledge that there are so many excellent fringe benefits. Weight loss, new friends, a better attitude, and a healthier you are just some of the extras you can expect from exercising your body and mind.

To get you going, let's find out where you are by starting with the *LIFEPLAN-NING* recreation quiz: Are You Intellectually, Culturally, and Physically Fit?

Are You Intellectually, Culturally, and Physically Fit?

To take this recreation test, simply follow the instructions for the five sections and honestly answer all the questions:

RECREATION/FITNESS

1. Do you participate in at least two sports or   Yes   No
forms of physical exercise on a regular basis?

2. Do you enjoy a level of proficiency in each of
these sports or exercises?   Yes   No

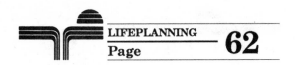

3. Do you participate in strenuous aerobic exercises at least three times per week?　　Yes　　No

4. Do you have a set time and schedule that you adhere to for exercise?　　Yes　　No

5. Can you run a mile and a half in less than 12-1/2 minutes?　　Yes　　No

RELAXATION RESPONSE

6. Do you eat lunch three times or more per week while continuing your work?　　Yes　　No

7. Do you find it difficult to do nothing?　　Yes　　No

8. Do you work on weekends and holidays as the rule instead of the exception?　　Yes　　No

9. Do you usually forego some of your allotted company vacation time each year because you're just too busy to get away?　　Yes　　No

10. Do you socialize more with work associates than any other groups of people?　　Yes　　No

11. Is your conversation dominated by thoughts of your work?　　Yes　　No

SOCIAL/CULTURAL

12. Have you attended a concert or the theater in the past three months?　　Yes　　No

13. Have you visited an art gallery/show or library in the past three months?　　Yes　　No

14. Have you seen a film (outside your

home) in the past two months? Yes No

15. Have you watched (on average) less than two hours of entertainment television on the nights you have been home during the past month? Yes No

16. Have you read a book, other than work-related in the past month? Yes No

INVOLVEMENT

17. Are you a member of a social organization that meets a minimum of 10 times a year? Yes No

18. Do you participate on a regular basis in an intellectual or cultural club, league, or organization? Yes No

19. Are you registered to vote? Yes No

20. Have you gotten involved in an endeavor that was completely new to you during the past six months? Yes No

ATTITUDE AND APPROACH TO LIFE

21. Do you often feel bored? Yes No

22. Do you find yourself at times wanting to be someone else? Yes No

23. If you had your life to live over again, would you want it to be dramatically different? Yes No

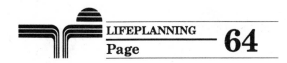

24. Do you regret having not learned certain
skills, like playing a musical instrument, speaking
a foreign language, or playing a sport, earlier in life
because it is too late to learn now?   Yes   No

25. Is the last dare you accepted long since
forgotten?   Yes   No

SCORING INSTRUCTIONS

For every YES answer in the FITNESS section
(Questions 1 through 5), you receive one point
                              FITNESS TOTAL   _____

For every NO answer in the RELAXATION
section (Questions 6 through 11), you receive one
point.
                              RELAXATION TOTAL   _____

For every YES answer in the SOCIAL section
(Questions 12 through 16), you receive one point.
                              SOCIAL TOTAL   _____

For every YES answer in the INVOLVEMENT section
(Questions 17 through 20), you receive one point.
                              INVOLVEMENT TOTAL _____

For every NO answer in the ATTITUDE section
(Questions 21 through 25), you receive one point.
                              ATTITUDE TOTAL   _____

TOTAL RECREATION SCORE   _____

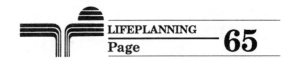

HOW TO INTERPRET YOUR SCORE

Your total score is important to record and save because it will be included in your overall **LIFEPLANNING** total and will help you analyze your status in the key areas of living. More will be said on this subject in Chapter Eight, The Balance.

For now, you should know that a total score of less than 16 means serious shortcomings in the area of recreation. As stated over and over again in **LIFEPLANNING**, tests work only as an indication of success or failure in an area, but a score of less than 16 is a strong indication that you are short-changing yourself.

Failing to adhere to a regular schedule of fitness can literally shortchange your health by cutting down the number of years you will live. Serious workaholic tendencies are evident in those of you failing the Relaxation Response part of the test. Too few positive answers in the Social/Cultural portion of the test mean that you are cheating yourself of life-enriching pastimes. A lack of yes answers to the Involvement questions too often means a lack of involvement in life, and too few points in the Attitude/Approach questions can mean too little faith in yourself.

To ensure a minimum level of participation in this important part of your life, you should be scoring 13 or higher. To score in the acceptable level, you should be in the 16 range, and the excellence level requires a score of 21 or more out of 25 points.

As always, the importance of the points is not the score but the quality of your life. According to a Gallup Poll published by *American Health* magazine, active, exercising adults are two-and-a-half times more likely than sedentary folks to say they are happy.

Let's now examine some additional ways to dramatically improve your chances for happiness through recreation.

THE LIFEPLANNING 10 COMMANDMENTS FOR INTELLECTUAL, CULTURAL, AND PHYSICAL FITNESS

This book attempts on every page to recognize the importance of the individual. In this section on recreation, that commitment continues and these commandments are provided with the understanding that each might mean something different to different people.

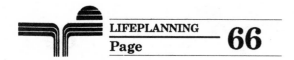

At the same time, it would be a rare case where the recreation commandments do not apply to everyone reading this book. For instance, swimming might be more appropriate for you than running, but the point of consistent, regular exercise should not be lost. The logic of applying all the recreation commandments in an individual manner is the key.

I. THOU SHALL LIMIT PASSIVE PARTICIPATION

The danger of spending too much time watching others compete rather than actively getting involved is discussed earlier in the chapter. It bears repeating. More than 40 percent of American adults over the age of 40 are overweight. With television watching and "doing nothing" our first and second favorite pastimes, it is no wonder.

This advice transcends athletics. While the importance of intellectual pursuits is also emphasized in this chapter, a common pitfall in this area is too many of us sit back and have entertainment spoon-fed to us. More will be said on this important subject in the remaining commandments, but the point is to get off your duff and engage your mind and body in active - not passive - participation.

II. THOU SHALL BECOME ACTIVE IN AN ORGANIZATION OR CLUB

Organizations are a great way to make new friends who share common interests. And a club or organization will do much of the legwork in organizing events, athletics, intellectual exchanges, or activities. Plus, organizations that meet on a regular basis provide motivation to stay actively involved.

There are several other good reasons to be involved in a club or organization that are best realized by visiting with current members or going through an orientation session.

There are thousands of fine organizations and clubs actively seeking new members and providing excellent opportunities for friendship, camaraderie, and new _opportunities_. Get started by finding out what other people with similar backgrounds to yours are involved in, or by taking your existing interests and finding out what sort of groups focus on those interests.

III. THOU SHALL KEEP THY PERSONAL LIFE DISTINCT FROM THY PROFESSIONAL LIFE

One of the quickest ways to identify a workaholic is to find someone who has friends only from his or her place of employment. The dangers of this limited

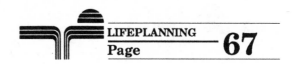

source of friends are obvious.

Having friends only from work means that often the only topic for discussion is work. Additionally, only having friends from work means having no outlet for diversified interests and discussions, and no opportunity to escape the day-to-day grind.

The other obvious pitfall is that additional strains are brought to bear on friendships by promotions, demotions, rewards, raises, and disciplinary actions. While some ongoing friendships from the workplace are healthy, you do not need the strain of this being your only pool of friends.

The other important point made by this commandment is that we are not our work. Rather, our work is an integral and important part of us, but only a part of the equation, not the definition. Already, we spend the better part of our waking day consumed by our work. It is important to have other diversions and escapes from that responsibility.

IV. THOU SHALL HAVE A DIVERSIFIED PROGRAM OF INTELLECTUAL RECREATION

Included in this chapter is a list of intellectual and cultural pursuits and a question on whether or not you are actively involved in one or more of these activities. If your answer was "yes," keep up the good work. If your answer was "no," the logical question is, "Why not?" Pure and simple, you are cheating yourself of a valuable and important part of your life.

A quick indicator of your life being out of balance is a "no" answer to the question, "Are you involved in intellectual pursuits beyond work?" By answering the "why not" of this question, you will identify the culprit that is stealing the little bit of time needed to address this key element of living. If you answered "too long" to the question of how long has it been since you last read a book, attended a play, or visited a museum, you have identified an important shortcoming in your life.

V. THOU SHALL NEVER STOP GROWING INTELLECTUALLY FIT

No, this is not a repeat of Commandment Four. The point of this commandment is to encourage ongoing learning. While the advice in Commandment Four can be most helpful, this commandment focuses more specifcally on the art of learning.

Too many of us feel that beyond our formal education and ongoing work-related education, we can shut down the part of our brain that is devoted to learning. Not

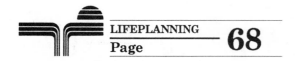

true. Like a muscle, the brain needs ongoing exercise in the form of challenge and stimulation if it is to avoid getting flabby.

While it is a medical fact that the brain shrinks with age, it is not necessary for your mental capabilities to wither away with time. If stimulation is ongoing in the form of reading, classes, discussion, and contemplation, you can continue your intellectual growth.

It is important that the mind and body both get ample forms of exercise.

VI. THOU SHALL ADHERE TO A SET ROUTINE OF AEROBIC EXERCISE

This commandment is a repeat of one of the health commandments but is repeated for a different reason. As documented in the health chapter, aerobic exercise is necessary for optimum health. It is listed in this chapter because aerobic exercise will facilitate all your recreational activities.

Feeling fit will provide you the necessary energy to participate in recreation and will keep you going long after others quit. Physical conditioning also will provide an edge to your ability to participate. Competitors on every level and in activities from golf to chess are realizing the importance of proper conditioning for staying mentally tough.

Our exercise revolution has even occurred in the workplace, as companies realize that employees in good shape are less prone to absenteeism, injury, and lapses of concentration. More and more employers are providing exercise facilities and classes to encourage staff members to get fit.

However or wherever you accomplish aerobic and physical conditioning, the point is to do it and feel better about yourself.

VII. THOU SHALL DEVELOP A LIFETIME APPROACH TO SPORTS AND FITNESS

The typical menu of sports played by teen-aged boys is lost to most of us in the adult world. Many of us spend the better part of our youth learning athletic skills that will, by and large, be unavailable to us as adults.

That is not to say that baseball, basketball, and football are not important to youngsters growing up. They develop motor skills, foster friendships, and provide important exercise and enjoyment. The point of this commandment is that along with the big three, it is important to develop athletic skills in sports that we can continue for a lifetime.

Running, swimming, cycling, golf, tennis, and bowling top that list. A little learning in those areas as a youngster can mean a lot later in life. No matter what

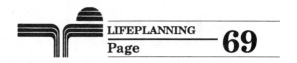

age you are, get involved with a sport that you enjoy and that provides you a lifetime of exercise.

VIII. THOU SHALL MAINTAIN A COMPLETE BUT CALM APPROACH TO COMPETITION

It is ironic that the vast majority of professional athletes rarely let their emotions show on the playing field, while the weekend duffer will explode with the slightest sign of imperfection.

The lesson, of course, is that professional athletes realize their maximum performance can only be delivered with their emotions in control. The time to show emotion, according to the world-class athlete, is after the touchdown is scored or the overhead smash is put away.

Weekend warriors will find that their athletic endeavors dramatically improve if they keep emotions in check. It's easier to find playing partners, too.

IX. THOU SHALL SEEK PROPER INSTRUCTION AND TEACHING

Tennis elbow is not the product of playing tennis. It is a byproduct of playing tennis improperly. Lower back pain or leg problems are not the result of playing golf or running. They are the result of swinging or running improperly. Poor scores or performances are not the fate of the Gods cast upon you. They are a direct correlation of your inability to execute, play, or participate properly.

If it is axiomatic that better scores and performances will improve personal attitude and enjoyment in athletics, it is also true that proper instruction and teaching will improve your scores and performance. The bottom line is get instruction or settle for less than the best on the playing field.

X. THOU SHALL NOT BORE OTHERS WITH INTELLECTUAL OR ATHLETIC ACHIEVEMENTS

Unless the Smithsonian Institute or *Sports Illustrated* deems your effort worthy for inclusion, you should be able to state your heroic accomplishments in one well-edited paragraph. If you do not, you are likely to be talking to an audience of one - you.

The obvious (and only) exception to Commandment 10 is when people all crazy about the same activity get together to talk about it. Even then, being long on listening and short on personal heroics will do much to endear you to others.

LIFEPLANNING LIBRARY
RECREATION

In the pages of the recreation chapter, we explore the myriad of ways a person can get involved in intellectual, cultural and athletic approaches to recreation. The many possibilities that exist would make any listing of recommended reading overwhelming. A better way to find reading to compliment your recreational pursuit is to ask your instructors or peers for recommendations.

If you are looking for a new form of recreation, try browsing through magazines. Typically, you will find a great selection of periodicals that will provide you a diversified menu of activities. Television programs, newspaper articles and videos can also serve the same purpose.

LIFEPLANNING LIBRARY RECOMMENDATIONS:

* Magazines
    — After many years of general interest publications like LIFE and LOOK, magazines began focusing on specific subjects and recreational pursuits are the big winner with hundreds of quality magazines surfacing on everything from surfing to personal computers. Happy browsing.

* USA TODAY
    — If you are curious about what the rest of the country is up to for work and play, there is no better source than the nation's only daily general interest newspaper.

* Television programs
    — Television is a great way to find out about activities so long as you eventually turn it off and personally participate.

* Local Newspaper
    — The daily record of activity in your area is found in your local newspaper. It should be mandatory reading.

* Recreation videos
    — A relatively new teaching tool that is second only to actual participation for getting involved.

CHAPTER FIVE

LIFEPLANNING: CAREER

V. CAREER

"No one knows what it is that he can do till he tries."

Publilius Syrus

Meet James, Zack, Tommy, and Ben. Athough brothers, each was unique in appearance, aptitude, and attitude. James was serious, studious, and preoccupied with gaining power within the family business. Zack was the antithesis of James. His interests ran to the outdoors and definitely away from the family business. Tommy, as the youngest, still was growing into manhood and was preoccupied with discovering the pleasures of the opposite sex and short-lived thrills. Ben, as the oldest, felt a paternal instinct toward Tommy and the family business, a kinship with the forthright Zack, and a brotherly tolerance of James.

As the years progressed, each continued to evolve in a pattern consistent with his personality. James pushed and pulled the strings as best he could to manipulate his and the company's fates. Zack left the business and his brothers to pursue an interest in ranching and raising horses. Tommy never grew up, even though he got married - over and over again. Ben put aside his love for architecture and redirected that intensity to the family and the family-owned manufacturing plant.

Tommy's future was all too predictable, as are most who fail to develop a career and seek to define themselves through a relationship. Ironically, James and Ben were to suffer a similar fate although for very different reasons. Both would find a fundamental frustration in life: James because he was trying to define himself through his work, and Ben because his well-intentioned but misguided love was never going to let him realize his vocational passion.

Simply put, James placed too much importance on work, Tommy too little, and Ben on everything else but his career. Only Zach, who left the family squabbling and a company he did not care for, found the career challenges and satisfaction we all need.

All in all, James, Zack, Tommy, and Ben turned out some disappointing statistics. Four brothers, one success story.

Sadly, many people fail to find the right line of work and, in turn, fail to realize the immense satisfaction of being matched up with the ideal career. Often, we end up in a career not because of a serious chain of conscious choices, but rather in spite of them.

The problem, of course, is not having a few jobs early in our career that are wrong for us. On average, Americans will work at approximately 10 jobs during their lifetime. This is a natural part of the process of better understanding ourselves and our vocational strengths and needs. The mistake is staying in a job after we realize it is wrong for us.

Why people stay in such a position varies. A good many young workers will take on too much consumer debt and become an indentured servant to bills and paychecks. Sometimes, family-related pressures will prevent people from leaving the security of a position they dislike for the unknown. Other workers will not budge because of fear. Judith M. Bardwick writes in her book, *The Plateauing*

THE AMERICAN WORKFORCE

THE TOP FIVE OCCUPATIONS BY AGE, SEX AND EDUCATION RANKED BY TOTAL NUMBER OF WORKERS

WOMEN 18+

1. Secretaries
2. Bookkeepers
3. Managers
4. Office Clerks
5. Nurses

MEN 18+

1. Managers
2. Manufacturing Supervisors
3. Truck Drivers
4. Small Business Owners
5. Sales

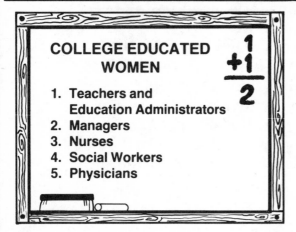

COLLEGE EDUCATED WOMEN

1. Teachers and Education Administrators
2. Managers
3. Nurses
4. Social Workers
5. Physicians

COLLEGE EDUCATED MEN

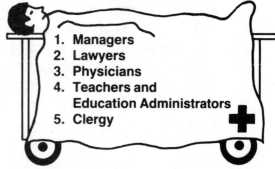

1. Managers
2. Lawyers
3. Physicians
4. Teachers and Education Administrators
5. Clergy

According to national averages from the Census Bureau the most widely held jobs by men and women and their average pay vary considerably by age, sex and educational level. How do you compare?

Category	Occupation	Compensation
Women 18+	Secretary	$10,622
Women College Educated*	Teacher	$16,094
Men 18+	Manager	$29,686
Men College Educated*	Manager	$38,915
YOU		$
	(Your Position)	(Your Income)

*Age 35 - 44/More than 4 years of college

Source: Census Bureau

Trap, "The pain of remaining has to become greater than the fear of changing."

The point of these pages is not that we should make capricious career changes. Instead, we should work hard to find the right work. If we encounter dead ends or roadblocks in our career paths, we should attempt to circumvent them through education and effort. If we wake up to the fact that we are mismatched in our jobs, we should methodically probe our skills, likes, and avenues of opportunity to find new, more satisfying lines of work.

There is certainly nothing wrong with working in the family business, and it is hard to fault people, like Ben, who give of themselves to help others. At the same time, we must continue seeking success in each key area of living and a balance among all of them.

In the best-selling book, *What Color is Your Parachute,* author Richard Nelson Bolles asks the reader to answer some simple questions: "If you could have any job in the world, what would it be? What do you want to do before you die?" He says the simplest answer is the best and that no study or test can match an honest answer to the question, "What do you really want to be?"

Before taking the following test, it is important you wrestle with that question and begin to formulate your answer. *LIFEPLANNING* concurs that no test, including this one, can tell you what to do with your life. A careful analysis of your skills, likes, and dislikes, plus some good old-fashioned soul searching is what is needed to help you determine your logical and desirable career path.

Most of us are called on to start making decisions that will shape our

---

WHAT MAKES WORK WORK FOR AMERICANS

How we react to our work environment depends on a variety of factors. In varying degrees, these are the elements that can make or break job satisfaction.

How do you rate yourself?

	Satisfied	Dissatisfied
Salary	_____	_____
Co-workers	_____	_____
Work Environment	_____	_____
Job Responsibility	_____	_____
Growth Potential	_____	_____
Promotion Potential	_____	_____
Resources/Equipment	_____	_____
Supervisor	_____	_____

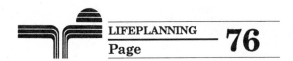
career paths at a young age. While our natural instincts many times will be strong enough to steer us in the proper direction, all too often the results are a mistake. The following test should be most helpful in aiding you to find out if you are in the right line of work and if your future is bright. As always, honesty is the key to getting a firm grip on your work status and future.

Start by answering the following questions.

Are You And Your Career Compatible?

This series of questions is designed to determine your current work status and future career prospects. Begin by answering each question as honestly as possible.

YOUR JOB ENVIRONMENT

1. I believe my co-workers like me.   True   False

2. My co-workers respect my work skills.   True   False

3. I have missed three or fewer days in the past year due to illness.   True   False

4. I have successfully demonstrated sufficient communication skills to convey and convince others of my ideas.   True   False

5. There are very few companies I would rather work for than mine.   True   False

YOUR WORK ATTITUDE

6. I do not enjoy my work.   True   False

7. I frequently daydream about retiring.   True   False

8. If I had my life to live over, I would choose another occupation.   True   False

9. I feel that I am not fairly paid for my work.   True   False

10. I have a negative attitude about my work.   True   False

THE FUTURE

11. The boss appreciates my work and has told me so in the past six months.　　True　　False

12. I received a larger pay increase during our last salary review than the other workers in my area of responsibility.　　True　　False

13. My boss would agree that I have the proper level of education and experience for the position I would assume if I were promoted.　　True　　False

14. I believe my future work opportunities are very good.　　True　　False

15. My last two performances reviews were positive.　　True　　False

16. My supervisor is likely to get promoted.　　True　　False

17. During the last 18 months, I have received an unsolicited inquiry about switching companies.　　True　　False

18. My supervisor's supervisor knows me and is aware of the quality of my work.　　True　　False

19. Throughout my career, I have demonstrated and held positions of leadership.　　True　　False

20. I have carefully thought through my career goals and have a plan of action to achieve them.　　True　　False

21. I understand my company's political power structure and pay attention to it.　　True　　False

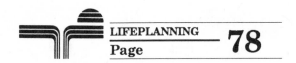

22. I voluntarily seek out information on my industry through trade publications and seminars.　　　　　　　　True　　　False

23. I am good at my work.　　　　　　　　True　　　False

24. I have a mentor in my company who has power.　　　　　　　　True　　　False

25. My instincts have steered me in the right direction repeatedly, and are to be trusted.　　　True　　　False

To figure your score for the career test, award points on the following basis: Two points for each True answer in the YOUR JOB ENVIRONMENT section.　　　　　　　_____

Two points for each False answer in the YOUR JOB ATTITUDE section.　　　　　　　_____

One point for each True answer in THE FUTURE section.　　　　　　　_____

Total score for the CAREER Test　　　=_____

HOW TO INTERPRET YOUR SCORE

The test on careers is divided into three sections. Each correctly answered question in "The Future" section receives one point, while the sections on "Your Work Attitude" and "Your Work Environment" carry additional weight because they are designed to find out if you are happy in your work. If you are not, you are in the wrong line of work or at the wrong company and, as stated earlier, you will spend entirely too much of your life being miserable. The section on "Your Job Environment" is designed to give a feel for how you fit in your work surroundings, and the final section, "The Future," is designed to help you determine if you can look forward to growth, challenges, and advancement.

For scoring purposes, a total of less than 19 means trouble in the workplace. It indicates you are not suited for the work, you're not fitting into the work environment, and subsequently you have a marginal future. A score of 26 or higher is acceptable but indicates you are not happy in your environment or not performing up to the standards of your boss. A score of 30 or higher means you are enjoying your work and are good at it - the combination we must all seek.

THE LIFEPLANNING 10 COMMANDMENTS FOR CAREER SATISFACTION

The following commandments represent common-sense and common-knowledge approaches to finding, keeping, and prospering in the career that's right for you. Whether you are a management trainee or the president of the company, these rules to work by will be helpful.

I. THOU SHALL SPEND YOUR CAREER DOING WHAT YOU ENJOY AND DO WELL

As stated in the body of this chapter and as is evident in the quiz, we spend so much of our life devoted to work that not enjoying it would be a type of torture no one should endure. At the same time, if we are not good at our work, it would be difficult to enjoy it over any length of time.

How you arrive at what work is best for you and what you do best should be an individual process. Examining your past successes and achievements, sophisticated career counseling, or plain old soul searching all can help you decide what's right for you.

The point, though, is to get there. Rarely will the world seek you out and hand you the job of your dreams, and too often we back into our career because of family pressures, misguided ideals and images, or, worse yet, coincidence. It is important we not let this happen.

Taking charge of your career path and growing through challenge and advancement will mean tremendous satisfaction that will carry over to all aspects of your life.

II. THOU SHALL INSIST ON GAINING, MAINTAINING, AND INCREASING THE KNOWLEDGE NEEDED IN THY WORK

The babysitting aspect of grade-school and high-school education coupled with the hard work necessary to complete college often leaves many of us sighing with

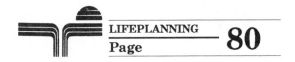

relief when our years of formal education are over. Unfortunately, the mistaken notion often accompanying this is that our learning days are behind us. This approach to learning will invariably stifle us in our careers if we let it persist.

A good example of the reluctance to learn has hit many people since the advent of the computer age. The application of the personal computer in the office is a relatively new phenomenon and requires education to utilize it. The continuing advancements in computers have caused them to permeate the office on every level. Ironically, the first to learn the advantages of the computer are secretaries, and the last to learn its many practical and time-saving applications are upper-level managers. The computer has created a power vacuum at the top.

The point, of course, is that anyone who avoids learning the advantages and applications of the computer runs the risk of being left out of the ultimate form of power-knowledge.

Aristotle succinctly explained man's curiosity when he said, "All men naturally desire to know." What he did not touch on was man's reluctance to invest the time and work to learn. Make sure you protect and enhance your future through the lifelong continuation of learning. This could be, for example, through company-provided schooling, continuing education, or reading work-related materials.

III. THOU SHALL UNDERSTAND THY STRENGTHS

Why does a person who is brilliant in math and a so-so communicator insist on being a lawyer? Why do children who hate working in the family business think that it will be OK as an adult? Why does a young woman who wants to help others through nursing let herself get pushed into hospital administration?

To avoid ending up in the wrong line of work, it is absolutely imperative that you catalog your skills, measure your past successes, and determine what is important to you. You must first and foremost know your strengths if you are to find your vocational calling.

Included in the list of strengths must be traits beyond technical skills. Some of the most important include:

- self-confidence
- communication skills
- enjoyment of one's work
- high energy
- setting goals
- a sense of humor
- being enjoyable to others
- pleasant appearance and good grooming.

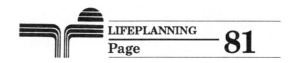

IV. THOU SHALL KNOW THY WEAKNESSES

Yes, you have them. Everyone does, and as a logical part of the process of finding and keeping the work that is right for you, you must know your weaknesses.

First, ask yourself why you cannot check off every positive trait listed in the commandment above and determine what it would take to gain those skills and traits. Review past failures and ask yourself what went wrong. What specifically could you have done differently to change the outcome of a project that failed? What pattern of criticism has followed you throughout your life? How do others see you? How do the following adjectives fit you: Honest, friendly, outgoing, contemplative, manipulative, positive, upbeat, conservative, pessimistic, attractive, intelligent, flexible, open-minded, sharing, lazy, hard-working?

Take the time to find out where you come up short and what it would take to improve. Remember, you can make as much progress by reducing or eliminating your shortcomings as you can by enhancing or improving your strengths.

V. THOU SHALL UNDERSTAND THY COMPANY'S POLITICS AND NOT PLAY THEM

A hard, cold fact of the business world is that politics are an inevitable part of every corporate structure. Choosing to ignore company politics will invariably be as fatal as getting too caught up in them. The proper approach is to understand that politics are a part of your work environment and to understand their dynamics. Practical ways to tune into politics but not be tainted by them are:

● Know the informal grapevine but avoid using it.

● Recognize the pockets of power and how the people that hold the power use and abuse it.

● Understand how you are characterized within the company, especially among the hierarchy.

● Be sensitive to the corporate culture. Every company has an informal set of rules of etiquette and survival. Abide by them.

● Be accessible and approachable, but avoid baring too much of your soul, your secrets, or your aspirations. There is a distinct difference between being paranoid and self-preservation.

● Develop a mentor relationship in both directions. Have someone higher up look after you and look after someone lower down in the company rank and file.

● Be sensitive to the question of age and rank. No greater creator of jealousy exists than young people on the rise or older people bogged down.

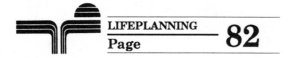
VI. THOU SHALL DEVELOP LISTENING SKILLS

This is a bit of advice that would serve everyone well in a host of personal and professional relationships. Listening seems to be a lost art and, sadly, is rarely taught in the business or educational environment.

To be a better listener, try relaxing and concentrating on what the speaker is saying as opposed to formulating your reply. Another important point is to focus on the message as opposed to the medium. Sometimes the person you are listening to may cloud the message with poor speaking habits, improper grammar, nervousness, or distracting mannerisms. Do your best to get past these obstacles to the speaker's point.

While few of us are capable (or gracious enough) to concentrate on 100 percent of the message being spoken to us, it is important to tune in on and comprehend the key points. While an important part of being a good listener is not interrupting, it is OK to once in a while ask for something to be repeated or explained. It will keep your speaker focused and flattered.

Finally, in a business environment, an important part of listening often includes taking notes.

VII. THOU SHALL TRUST THY INSTINCTS

Webster says that instinct is the natural feeling or sense of what is correct or effective. *LIFEPLANNING* agrees and goes a step further to say that instinctive action in the workplace is the sixth sense we develop for a situation even though we might not have encountered that exact set of circumstances.

It is difficult at best to guide someone concerning when and how to use instinctive action, other than to advise that ultimately all decision-making requires a degree of it. After researching the question at hand and getting the appropriate input, it comes time to make the decision and then live with and support your decision. Trust your instincts. They are usually right.

VIII. THOU SHALL NOT PROCRASTINATE

In the commandment above, you are advised to gather up the necessary information to answer a question and then answer it. Procrastinating only adds an unnecessary worry and distraction to an issue.

On the subject of procrastination, famous author Napoleon Hill wrote, "The way to develop decisiveness is to start right where you are, with the very next question you face." *LIFEPLANNING* adds that to best avoid procrastination, priortize your projects on paper with reasonable goals and deadlines. Pad your schedule based on your experiences to allow for the daily emergencies and interruptions we all encounter. Finally, stick to your goals and priority outline.

In case you are still not convinced that procrastination is costly, see what your time is worth.

The following chart calculates the actual hourly cost of time for people at various income levels. The value of each of your hours - even each of your minutes - is something to consider if you are considering procrastinating. It is also worthwhile information to remember every time a meeting or phone call runs long or you run late.

Salary/ Year (Plus 40% for benefits)	Value Per Hour	Value Per Minute
$ 10,000	$ 6.73	$0.11
12,000	8.08	0.13
15,000	10.10	0.17
20,000	13.46	0.22
25,000	16.83	0.28
30,000	20.19	0.34
40,000	26.92	0.45
50,000	33.65	0.56
60,000	40.38	0.67
70,000	47.12	0.79
80,000	53.85	0.90
90,000	60.58	1.01
100,000	67.31	1.12

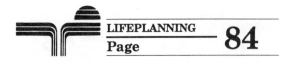

IX. THOU SHALL HAVE BOTH SHORT- AND LONG-TERM GOALS

When driving to a new place, most of us review a map and figure out stops along the way that will lead us to our ultimate destination. We establish short- and long-term goals for the trip.

Life should be treated no differently. We should take a careful look at where we want to end up in life and how logically we can get there.

If the goal you set is to earn a particular position and a level of income so that you can retire at a specific age, you have established some important long-term goals. Next, you need to determine the logical sequence of reaching those ultimate goals. What sort of positions and salaries will you need to earn along the way? Your next step is to determine what type of projects and successes you will need to earn for promotions and raises. To best accomplish that goal, you will have to determine the basic skills, experiences, and education necessary to get a foot in the door and a start on those projects.

Like reading a road map, you start at the destination and work your way back toward the starting point, all along the way establishing the shorter term destinations that will guide you.

Professional golfers often use this reverse technique. While preparing to tee off, they imagine themselves on the green looking back at their starting point, the tee. They take this new perspective, calculate the percentages of various shots, and chart the proper route for their particular abilities.

Life's goals can be attained in much the same way. Determine where it is you want to go, and then figure out the logical way to get there. Remember, it is much easier getting there when you know where it is you want to go.

X. THOU SHALL ENJOY AS YOU GO

A good many Americans are living for tomorrow at the expense of today. Some examples: The father who works so hard he neglects his children today so he can give them all the best tomorrow; the woman who devotes her life to a career she hates so she can be adequately financed in her latter years; people who neglect recreational or cultural pursuits until later in life because they are just too busy now.

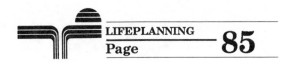
Maintaining a balance in life does not mean sacrificing time with your children, devoting a large part of your life to work that does not suit you, or indefinitely postponing recreation. Rarely has sacrificing everything today helped tomorrow.

Please do not misunderstand this advice. Yes, we must all save, work, and plan for tomorrow, but those efforts should not be done in a manner that destroys today.

The main message in *LIFEPLANNING* - balance in life - means that enjoyment and fulfillment are possible throughout life, and are not just reserved for a small portion of it.

LIFEPLANNING LIBRARY
CAREER

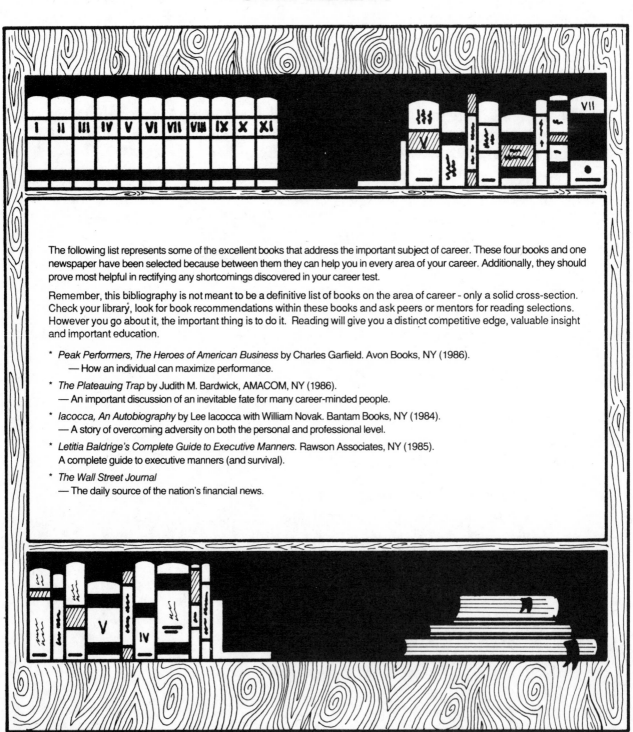

The following list represents some of the excellent books that address the important subject of career. These four books and one newspaper have been selected because between them they can help you in every area of your career. Additionally, they should prove most helpful in rectifying any shortcomings discovered in your career test.

Remember, this bibliography is not meant to be a definitive list of books on the area of career - only a solid cross-section. Check your library, look for book recommendations within these books and ask peers or mentors for reading selections. However you go about it, the important thing is to do it. Reading will give you a distinct competitive edge, valuable insight and important education.

* *Peak Performers, The Heroes of American Business* by Charles Garfield. Avon Books, NY (1986).
    — How an individual can maximize performance.

* *The Plateauing Trap* by Judith M. Bardwick, AMACOM, NY (1986).
    — An important discussion of an inevitable fate for many career-minded people.

* *Iacocca, An Autobiography* by Lee Iacocca with William Novak. Bantam Books, NY (1984).
    — A story of overcoming adversity on both the personal and professional level.

* *Letitia Baldrige's Complete Guide to Executive Manners.* Rawson Associates, NY (1985).
    A complete guide to executive manners (and survival).

* *The Wall Street Journal*
    — The daily source of the nation's financial news.

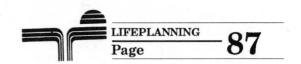

CHAPTER SIX

LIFEPLANNING: COMPANIONSHIP

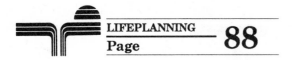

VI. COMPANIONSHIP

"No sooner met but they looked, no sooner looked than they loved, no sooner loved than they sighed, no sooner sighed but they asked one another the reason, no sooner knew the reason but they sought the remedy."

William Shakespeare
"As You Like It"

Meet Elizabeth. Educated at Smith College, the daughter of a prominent stockbroker, she was both familiar and comfortable with the finer things in life. Her idea of roughing it was wearing L. L. Bean to a picnic in the park. A member in good standing in the Junior League, she spent considerable time helping people she had never met. Everything about Elizabeth was likeable and she had many friends. If anyone had anything negative to say about her, it was that she was too perfect and was not crazy about children.

Meet Lee. A journalism graduate from the University of Missouri, he spent his days as an investigative reporter for a major daily newspaper and his weekends banging around in the country four-wheeling. His father, a traveling salesman, died when Lee was still in college, and ever since then, he had been preoccupied with having his own family. His love for the outdoors and camping would make him a popular father, but his wife was not interested in starting a family. His wife was Elizabeth.

The old saying "as different as night and day" is most appropriate in describing Elizabeth and Lee. How they got together was still a mystery to their friends even though the two of them remember well how they fell in love during college. She was rebounding from a disastrous relationship and his serious side appealed to her. He was serious primarily because his father had just passed away. She appealed to him because she was organized and little else was organized in his life at that moment. It was ironic that they could make a decision of the magnitude of marriage when they were barely old enough to vote, no banker would loan them money, and their most important decisions to date were the electives they selected in college.

Of course, most people pick partners for life when they have had little experience in life. The majority of marriages take place before the age of 25. Unfortunately, we are nearing the point when the majority of marriages end in divorce. Approximately half of all marriages currently end in disaster and the statistics, while showing some signs of stabilizing, still leave the United States with a high rate of divorce and a sizable number of newly single people. The two trends probably most responsible for slowing the divorce rate are that many marriages are occurring later and those who are married are not giving up so easily.

Happily, Lee and Elizabeth decided not to give up too easily on their marriage and are proceeding cautiously. With the help of a professional marriage counselor, they are dealing with the early days of their relationship as well as their current incompatabilities.

Elizabeth has not become an overnight camper but is dealing in a very honest way with the question of having children. Lee realizes how important Elizabeth's charity work is and is more supportive. In addition to opening the lines of

THE NEW LOOK OF THE AMERICAN HOUSEHOLD

MEDIAN AGE FOR FIRST MARRIAGES

1986 Men — 25.7

1970 Men — 23.2

1986 Women — 23.1

1970 Women — 20.8

PERSONS LIVING ALONE

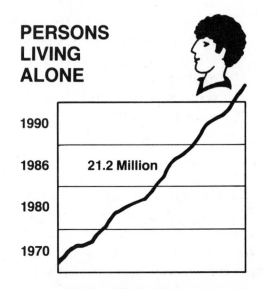

1990	
1986	21.2 Million
1980	
1970	

UNMARRIED COUPLES LIVING TOGETHER

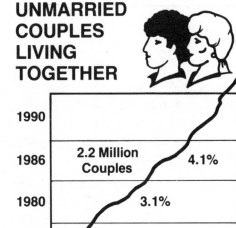

1990	
1986	2.2 Million Couples — 4.1%
1980	3.1%
1970	1.2%

TRADITIONAL FAMILIES AS A PERCENT OF U.S. HOUSEHOLDS

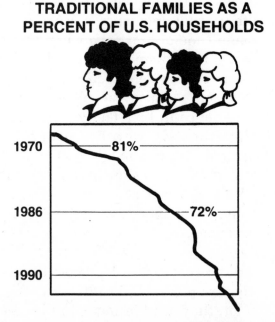

1970	81%
1986	72%
1990	

Source: Census Bureau

communication and sharing some common interests, they are learning how to laugh again. A sure sign of trouble in love is a couple losing their sense of humor.

Since this chapter is about companionship in all types of situations, as opposed to just marriage, we will move on to the test of your likeability and loveability. We will also provide some valuable information on how to more than survive, to thrive, in all types of relationships.

A final word on the subject of relationships, friendships, companionship, marriage, and mates before we begin the test. No amount of money, health, or success can take the place or

---

AMERICA'S PET PALS

Relationships, friendships, and family are important to our well-being, and every person should strive for healthy relationships throughout life. Another source of comfort and companionship can come from pets.

Some medical studies suggest that pets can have a therapeutic value. More importantly, any pet owner can tell you that pets provide love, comfort, and laughter.

America's two favorite pets are cats (56 million) and dogs (51 million).

Source: MRCA Information

---

importance of having friends, and true friendship is all too often an elusive commodity.

When found, it must be nurtured and looked after constantly and consistently. Most importantly, it must be treasured and respected. Few authors have said it better or more succinctly than Ralph Waldo Emerson in *Friendship*, when he wrote, "the only way to have a friend is to be one." Let's see what kind of friend you are by answering the following questions.

ARE YOU LIKEABLE? LOVEABLE? HUGGABLE?

COMPANIONSHIP

To find out the answers to the three important questions posed in the title of this test, please answer the questions in the following four sections. To provide a degree of objectivity, decide if your friends would agree with your answers. Please be as honest as possible.

THE MIRROR

Understanding how you relate to others starts with finding out how you feel about yourself. Do you believe and would the people in your life agree that:

1. I am an attractive person. True False

2. I have an optimistic outlook on life. True False

3. I do not worry about details I have no control over. True False

4. While I enjoy the company of others, being alone from time to time is important to me. True False

5. I feel criticism is important for my growth and I am not afraid of it. True False

6. I have both casual and intimate friendships. True False

7. I receive love and friendship back in amounts reasonably equal to that I give out. True False

8. I think that life has been fair to me. True False

9. I have a friend (other than my spouse) with whom I can confide about my failures, fears, hopes, and dreams. True False

10. I will continue to grow and prosper in the future. True False

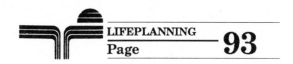

FRIENDS, FAMILY, AND FEELINGS

No better measure of your likeability and loveability exists than the friendship and love you give and receive from friends and family. To find out how you are doing, please answer the following questions:

11. Are you married?   Yes   No

12. Do you have children?   Yes   No

13. Do you have a diversity of friends,
young, old, and both sexes?   Yes   No

14. Are you involved in civic or charitable
work (what is it)?   Yes   No

15. Have you gone out of your way in the past
three months to perform an uncalled-for act of
kindness (recall the specific event)?   Yes   No

YOUR WORLD

How you treat others besides friends says a great deal about you as a person. Answer the following questions based on how you actually deal with the world around you:

16. When I hear of the success of
friends I typically feel

1. pride.
2. jealousy.
3. disinterest.

17. In conversations I most often

1. listen carefully.
2. look for opportunity to make my point.
3. feign interest and concentrate on other matters.

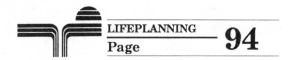

18. In dealing with people I am meeting for the first time, I find I usually

1. wait and let their actions determine my feelings toward them.
2. quickly categorize them so they are easier to deal with.
3. wait to determine my reaction to them after I find out what they can do for me.

19. I have made friends with people other than business associates

1. frequently.
2. never.
3. seldom.

20. I use common courtesy in dealing with everyone including my spouse

1. always.
2. occasionally.
3. never.

LOVE AND FRIENDSHIP IN ACTION

How we treat our friends, family, and ourselves is another excellent indication of our "likeability quotient." The following questions provide a snapshot of how you actually conduct this important part of your life. Do not answer the questions casually. For each question answer Yes or No. To insure honesty, recall the specific event.

21. In the past 10 weeks, I have written a letter to a friend and have both discussed and inquired about personal matters.   Yes   No

22. In the past 10 weeks, I have received a letter from a friend.   Yes   No

23. In the past 10 weeks, I have attended a party of a non-business nature that celebrated a special occasion for a friend or family member. (Christmas should not be counted. Birthdays, anniversaries, or announcements should be).   Yes   No

24. In the past year, friends or family members have held a party for me celebrating a special date (birthday, anniversary, promotion, or achievement all can be included).   Yes   No

25. In the event of an emergency, do you have two friends who would loan you $500, no questions asked and on a moment's notice? (The friends should not be family members or a banker}.   Yes   No

26. Do you actually participate in and enjoy conversations that do not include areas of personal knowledge, expertise, or interest?   Yes   No

27. Do you believe in God?   Yes   No

28. Do you have an active, loving, sexual relationship on an ongoing basis with a loving, caring partner?   Yes   No

29. Do you have a fulfilling, satisfying, and enjoyable sex life that includes the four stages of lovemaking (foreplay, intercourse, orgasm, afterplay)?   Yes   No

30. Do you have significant friendships with people of both sexes?   Yes   No

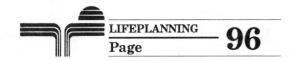

SCORING INSTRUCTIONS

For every Yes answer in the MIRROR section,
you receive one point.   _____

For every Yes answer in the FRIENDS, FAMILY,
AND FEELINGS section, you receive two points.   _____

For every number 1 answer in the YOUR
WORLD section, you receive one point.   _____

For every Yes answer in the LOVE AND
FRIENDSHIP section, you receive one point.   _____

Enter here the total for the four sections
YOUR COMPANIONSHIP SCORE   _____

HOW TO INTERPRET YOUR SCORE

How did you do? Probably not as well as you thought you would. Most people see themselves as the perfect partner or pal, when in reality, we all could improve our relationships dramatically with a little effort.

To get down to the nitty-gritty, you should know that a score of less than 19 means you are probably not succeeding in the area of companionship. Now do not overreact and start rationalizing your low score with the fact that you are married, have children, are liked at the office, and have a regular golf four-some. It is possible to have all of those elements yet still have a low score. The low score is an indicator that your friends and family are putting out more than you are giving. In other words, you can do better. More on how in a moment.

If you scored around 26, you are in the acceptable range but in need of some extra effort. A score of 30 means you are on target with your approach to relationships and should keep up the good work.

In addition to your overall score, the specific sections of the test can be very enlightening. A low score in "The Mirror" section can indicate low self-esteem and a pessimistic attitude towards life. The "Friends, Family and Feelings" section is a measure of your involvement with others. How you treat others besides your circle of friends says a great deal about you as a person. The "Your World" questions and more importantly your answers should provide some insight on your patience, interest, and courtesy to others.

The final section on "Love and Friendship in Action" is a quick way to catalog what you are doing for others and how they are responding. More can be found on analyzing your Companionship score in relationship to your other scores in the chapter, The Balance.

THE LIFEPLANNING 10 COMMANDMENTS OF COMPANIONSHIP

Few things in life are worth more than good friends, strong family ties, and a loving partner. How each of us go about obtaining and maintaining these types of relationships is always going to be individual in nature, but the following 10 commandments will prove invaluable in developing healthy, growing relationships for all of us.

I. THOU SHALL BE A GOOD LISTENER

This commandment is listed here and in the Career chapter for the simple reason that listening makes for success in business or pleasure. Sadly, it is rarely taught as a skill in either environment.

To be a better listener, try relaxing and concentrating on what the speaker is saying as opposed to formulating your reply. Another important point is to focus on the message as opposed to the medium. Sometimes the person you are listening to may cloud the message with poor speaking habits, improper grammar, nervousness, or distracting mannerisms. Do your best to get past this to the speaker's point.

Finally, while few of us are capable (or gracious enough) to concentrate on 100% of the message being spoken, it is important to tune in on and comprehend the key points. While an important part of being a good listener is not interrupting, it is OK to once in a while ask for something to be repeated or explained. This will keep your speaker focused and flattered.

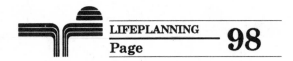

II. THOU SHALL GIVE CRITICISM IN A
POSITIVE, NURTURING MANNER

Disraeli said, "It is much easier to be critical than correct." *LIFEPLANNING* says that if you are going to be critical, you had better be correct. You also had better be cautious, kind, and gentle. Any of you who have been through the experience of trying to teach a mate an athletic or technical skill have probably learned how difficult the art of teaching can be. A new and shared skill is being developed as the relationship progresses, and while at times criticism is a fundamental part of building that relationship, if not handled carefully, it can be destructive. A few good rules to follow when you feel the urge to critique are:
- Determine your motivation before speaking.
- Be honest when it is constructive and quiet when it is cruel.
- Be positive - not pious. Remember, no one is perfect, including you.
- Communicate, communicate, communicate.

III. THOU SHALL ACCEPT CRITICISM WITH AN OPEN MIND

The adage that "it is better to give than to receive" is especially true when it comes to criticism. In all fairness, though, it is important that we be able to handle both the giving and receiving ends of criticism in a relationship. To deal with criticism in the best way possible, please reread Commandments 1 and 2.

IV. THOU SHALL REMEMBER THE LITTLE THINGS

Whether we are talking about a husband/wife relationship, two pals, or a boss and secretary, it is important that both parties remember that while the big things create the relationship, the little things define it. Additionally, the little things, if left unattended, can sour the core of the relationship.

Any discussion or attempt to define the "little things" in a relationship is to risk being trite and sounding corny. In general, though, remember the nicknames and extra efforts from early in your relationship. For heaven's sake, do not forget birthdays, anniversaries, or acts of kindness. Finally, compliment others when they look nice, thank them when they go out of their way for you, and do not be afraid to do something nice for absolutely no reason other than the joy of it.

V. THOU SHALL HUG, CUDDLE, AND COMFORT

The comfort of a mother's hug, the sense of security in a father's arms, the intimacy of a lover's embrace. Touching and being held is as important to our spiritual well-being as food is to our body's nourishment. Do not be afraid to give or accept physical affection - when appropriate, kiss, hold hands, hug.

VI. THOU SHALL SHARE THE POSITIVES
AND THE NEGATIVES

Mind reading is at best a difficult if not lost art. Do not force your friends or family to attempt it with you. People who do not share their feelings run the risk of having others do the same to them. The flip side of this is the friend or mate who demands too much.

While striking an emotional balance in friendships and relationships is never easy, it can become impossible without communication. At the risk of oversimplification, the best advice is to talk. Talk both about the feelings you're experiencing and the cause of your feelings. In turn, if your friend or partner is hurting or in need, listen to the problem and help the person understand the cause. The silent treatment should always be considered out-of-bounds in a relationship.

The bottom line is that each person represents a different collection of experiences, emotions, and methods of showing them. In every relationship, we must strive to understand this balance through conversation, and understand too when a person simply needs to be left alone.

VII. THOU SHALL WORK TO ALWAYS LOOK THY BEST

Statistically, it is a fact that taller men and women have a better chance of succeeding in business. Several studies also have proven that better-looking people have an improved chance of making friends, earning promotions, and gaining peer approval.

Whether we like it or not, appearance is important, and while there is little we can do about our height, we have a great deal of control over our appearance. Our attention (or lack of attention) to detail in our appearance is a statement to the world, and it is naive to think that people we encounter will not have their reaction to us tempered by how we appear to them. How we dress, our grooming habits, and our general demeanor are absolutely essential elements of our personalities.

The appearance of an East Coast broker and a West Coast movie producer will typically be very different, yet both could be successful in their own right. For this reason it is best to emulate those you admire rather than adhere to some dogma about dressing for success. Ultimately, some blend of what works in your peer group and profession, coupled with your individual touches, should help you develop a distinctive look. Good grooming is also an integral part of the mix. Never underestimate its importance.

A final note on appearance goes to those who are in an ongoing relationship. Pretend that "til death do us part" also applies to keeping up good grooming, because nothing will kill a relationship quicker than taking your mate or your appearance for granted.

VIII. THOU SHALL HAVE REALISTIC EXPECTATIONS IN THY RELATIONSHIPS

The statistics are numbing. Half of the women today have difficulty reaching orgasm, and more than 30 percent have lost interest in sex altogether. As many as half of all married women and six out of 10 married men been involved in at least one extra-marital affair. On the flip side, there are estimates that as high as 5 percent of all married couples have never experienced sexual intercourse, and approximately half of all marriages today end in divorce. In the face of these overwhelming statistics, a stable, sexually active, and fulfilling marriage may seem an elusive commodity. It is, and the career demands and social pressures that burden marriage show no signs of letting up.

In light of these odds, pessimism might seem more logical than realism, but it's not. When people meet and fall in love, they determine that all those statistics and horror stories are what happen to other people, not them.

To enhance a marriage's chance of success and avoid these common pitfalls, one simple rule should be followed, "Do not marry strangers." This doesn't mean you shouldn't marry someone new to you, or that you must marry someone you grew up with. It means that regardless of how you meet someone, you should invest a great deal of time getting to know that person to avoid becoming an unpleasant statistic.

The attitude every couple should live with is not that it could never happen to us, but rather that we must work hard to ensure that our relationship will last. The best first step - be realistic. A good next step is to continue communicating.

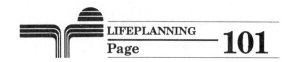

Finally, never lose your sense of humor. If you can size up your problems, talk about them, and continue to laugh through the challenges, you are a long way towards solving them.

IX. THOU SHALL SEEK INTIMATE FRIENDSHIPS AS WELL AS PROFESSIONAL FRIENDSHIPS

The first eight commandments in this chapter on companionship deal with how to get along in friendship or marriage. Often, the rules are the same. In Commandment IX, the advice goes in an opposite direction. How you best succeed in business is to minimize the intimacy of your relationships and keep your work associates on a friendly, but professional, level. This is almost in direct contrast to how you deal with intimate relationships.

It is important to remember that work relationships are dramatically influenced by the dynamics of the power and influence structure within the business. The business associates with whom you believe to be good friends are often friendly only because of potential gain. It would be paranoid to make too much of this reality, but to be practical, our lasting relationships should typically be sought outside the workplace.

X. THOU SHALL GIVE EVERYTHING AND THEN GIVE A LITTLE MORE

Athletes call this giving 110 percent. *LIFEPLANNING* calls it imperative to the survival of a relationship. Throughout this chapter, the overwhelming odds against a relationship succeeding are well-documented. To avoid becoming a statistic, give everything you've got, and then give a little more.

LIFEPLANNING LIBRARY
COMPANIONSHIP

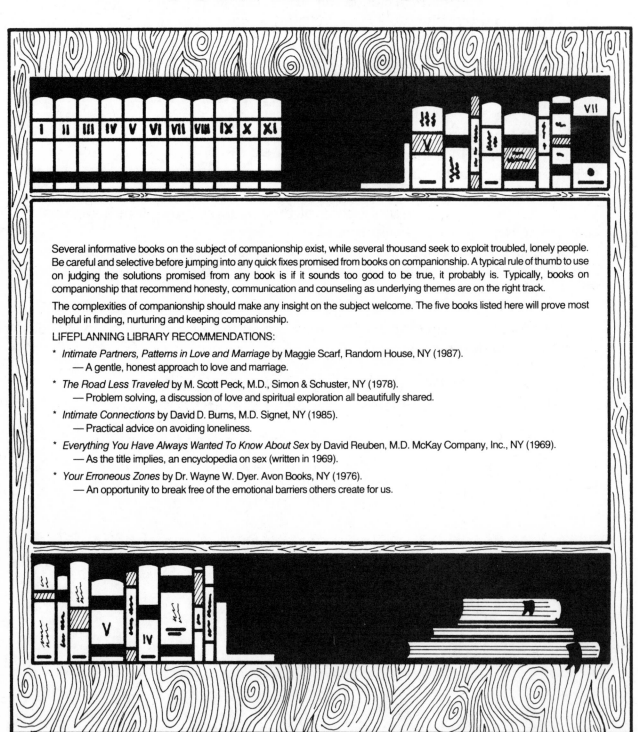

Several informative books on the subject of companionship exist, while several thousand seek to exploit troubled, lonely people. Be careful and selective before jumping into any quick fixes promised from books on companionship. A typical rule of thumb to use on judging the solutions promised from any book is if it sounds too good to be true, it probably is. Typically, books on companionship that recommend honesty, communication and counseling as underlying themes are on the right track.

The complexities of companionship should make any insight on the subject welcome. The five books listed here will prove most helpful in finding, nurturing and keeping companionship.

LIFEPLANNING LIBRARY RECOMMENDATIONS:

* *Intimate Partners, Patterns in Love and Marriage* by Maggie Scarf, Random House, NY (1987).
    — A gentle, honest approach to love and marriage.

* *The Road Less Traveled* by M. Scott Peck, M.D., Simon & Schuster, NY (1978).
    — Problem solving, a discussion of love and spiritual exploration all beautifully shared.

* *Intimate Connections* by David D. Burns, M.D. Signet, NY (1985).
    — Practical advice on avoiding loneliness.

* *Everything You Have Always Wanted To Know About Sex* by David Reuben, M.D. McKay Company, Inc., NY (1969).
    — As the title implies, an encyclopedia on sex (written in 1969).

* *Your Erroneous Zones* by Dr. Wayne W. Dyer. Avon Books, NY (1976).
    — An opportunity to break free of the emotional barriers others create for us.

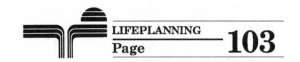
CHAPTER SEVEN

LIFEPLANNING: GEOGRAPHY

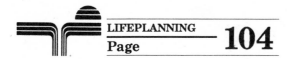

VII. GEOGRAPHY

"'Mid pleasures and palaces though we may roam,
be it ever so humble, there's no place like home."

John Howard Payne
Home, Sweet, Home

Meet yourself.

Unlike previous chapters, where we have introduced you to people with problems, challenges, and backgrounds that may or may not be similar to yours, this chapter focuses directly on you. In this section, we'll pose a series of questions that should be helpful in determining the appropriate regions of the country for you to live.

This chapter differs from the previous chapters in other ways as well. The questions do not accumulate points or ultimately contribute to your *LIFEPLANNING* score, and this chapter does not contain any *LIFEPLANNING* commandments. Pure and simple, we work to qualify your likes, dislikes, interests, and vocational needs to find out if your address and personality are compatible.

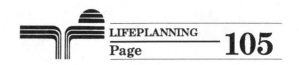

To infuse a dose of reality into this discussion, let's start with some background on why people live where they do.

Typically, the main reason people live in a particular area is coincidence - most of us end up living in the general area of our birth. In fact, the vast majority of Americans live their life within a 100-mile radius of their place of birth. What's more, only approximately one in five people move when they retire, even though this group is certainly free to relocate.

After the birth factor is taken into consideration, the next largest determinant of where we choose to live is our work. According to the April 1987 issue of *American Demographics* , about 60 percent of the approximately 40 million people who move each year relocate within their same county. The majority of the people relocating longer distances are doing so to move to a job or in search of one.

Of course, there is nothing inherently wrong with wanting to live where we were raised, around friends, family, and familiar places. It is OK and practical to live where our company transfers us.

What is not OK is living in a city we dislike when the only reason we're there is because it is where we happened to be born or transferred. Few things in life can cause as much discomfort as living in a city or area that makes us miserable.

The following questions and graphic materials are designed to help you help yourself through the process of determining the right part of the country for your likes, interests, and background. The questions are designed to facilitate this process, as well as help you know yourself better. *LIFEPLANNING* has resisted the temptation to determine the perfect place for you to live through a process of qualifying questions. That type of formula approach has too many pitfalls. As stated earlier, a better way to determine where you should reside is through an intelligent review of your likes, interests, and background, coupled with personal visits to the various areas of the country.

Let's get started by cataloging any restrictions you might have because of family, health, occupation, or strong likes or dislikes:

1. Do you or your spouse insist on living near certain family members or friends?

2. Does anyone in your household have any restrictions on where they can live due to a health condition?

3. Are you or your spouse tied to a particular area of the country because of your work?

4. Do you or your mate insist on living in a particular area of the country?

Any Yes answers to the first four questions will, by and large, cut this chapter short. A Yes answer means you are highly restricted in where you can or will live. The best course of action for you to pursue can be found in the previous chapters on how to improve your life regardless of where you live.

For those of you who are not restricted, continue with the following questions. Read each question carefully. Think through your immediate reaction to the question. Go on to read the comment.

1. Do you want to live someplace else?

Comment: No question in this chapter is more important than this one. If you answered Yes, the next logical question is why? And the next logical action is careful research and investigation into alternative places to live.

2. Why do you want to move?

_____ improve social life   _____ start over
_____ solve a problem   _____ dislike job

Comment: Understanding your motivation for wanting to move is very important. Understanding that potential trouble can be found in any of these answers is also important. Any of these motivations potentially indicates a problem or shortcoming in your life that moving rarely addresses. Typically, the problem or shortcoming tags along with the move. While a move can improve your social life, eliminate a problem or give you a fresh start, it is always best to resolve any problems prior to moving rather than running away from them.

3. Do you wish to live in a different climate?

Comment: This can be an excellent goal. Living in a climate that is compatible with your personality, recreational interests, and preference is a tremendous way to boost quality of life. At the same time, we should all realize that every climate has its positive and negative aspects. For instance, Phoenix has glorious sun-drenched winters but more than 150 days a year with temperatures higher than 90 degrees. Maui is paradise until you check out the cost of living. The point is that paradise on earth does not exist, and if it did, it would fill up fast. A final note on climate is to make sure you are comfortable with the negative aspects of a climate before moving there. To some, the New England winters are more tolerable than Florida's humidity or the desert's scorching summers. Understand your preferences.

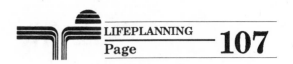

4. Do you make new friends easily?

   Comment: This question and your answer are important since a move always involves developing a new social circle. If you are not adept at this, or if meeting your current friends took a long time, be cautious about moving. Loneliness can quickly sour the rewards of a new job or the allure of a better climate.

5. Have you traveled extensively and personally visited the place you want to move to?

   Comment: The absolute best way to determine the right place for you to live is through a process of elimination. Once you visit, explore, and educate yourself on the area, you can best judge if it is right for you. Unfortunately, this is not always practical. Use your vacations to visit new places, and go through the checklist of what is right and wrong with a particular area. This is especially good advice for those of you who are convinced you would like to move when you retire. Investigate now.

6. What are your recreational and cultural interests?

Winter Activities

_____ skiing
_____ sledding
_____ ice fishing
_____ ice skating

Water Related Activities

_____ fishing
_____ water skiing
_____ scuba diving
_____ sailing

Warm Weather Activities

_____ golf
_____ tennis
_____ hiking
_____ camping
_____ sunbathing

Cultural Activities

_____ ballet
_____ movies
_____ concerts
_____ museums
_____ theater

Sporting Activities

_____ baseball
_____ football
_____ hockey
_____ soccer
_____ basketball

Social Activities

_____ bridge/cards
_____ dancing
_____ clubs
_____ crafts
_____ hobbies

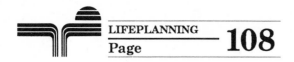
Comment: If your interests do not match up with the available facilities or climate, you are not going to be happy. The tremendous amount of information and statistics available from Chamber of Commerces, potential employers, weather bureaus, etc. should keep any area from being a mystery. The personal visit also will give you a chance to investigate. Ask lots of questions about an area. In summation, review the activities you enjoy. Prioritize them as essential to your happiness or only of mild interest. Then research any area you're considering. It will be time well spent.

7. Can you afford to live there?

Comment: The first part of your answer is not related to cost of living but rather to making a living. Is your line of work available in the area you are interested in, and if so, what are your chances of finding a good position? After researching that question through headhunters, business, and personal contacts, and some diligent research, you have to ask yourself if you can afford to live there in the style you are accustomed. As an example, New York is an excellent place to build a career in publishing or finance, but for a management trainee, costs can be prohibitive. There are several indexes available that will give you an idea of the adjustments you would have to make because of cost-of-living differences. Before relocating, explore them.

8. Do you want to get away from it all?

Comment: We have all fantasized about the log cabin in the mountains or the beachhouse on the ocean, but how many of us would actually chuck it all for such a dream? These fantasies serve as an important safety valve, though, and are an important means of dealing with and escaping from daily pressures. Another important purpose fantasies serve is to help us identify qualities that are important to us. Someone who dreams about life in a log cabin obviously has an affinity for the outdoors. Since it is impractical for most of us to actually leave it all behind for the cabin, we can

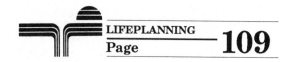

appease the fantasy by living close to an area that makes camping, hiking, four-wheeling, or other outdoor activities easily accessible. The point is to listen to our fantasies and feed them with some of our day-to-day activities, including the place we live.

9. Do you define yourself by your address?

   Comment: The only correct answer to this question is yes, no and maybe. Yes, in that where we live does in part define us, but only in part. As stated earlier, our address should be compatible with our likes, interests, and vocation, and that is too strong a tie to not be a part of our personality. No, in that we must ultimately avoid totally defining ourself by our locale. Why? It simply is too self-limiting. Everyone who lives in Green Bay is not football crazy and everybody in California is not into surfing. Maybe, because the address as a part of who you are applies sometimes and sometimes it does not. Ideally, we should all have the good fortune to live in an area that complements us as a person but does not complicate our effort to be an individual.

After reviewing the preceding questions in this chapter and discussing your thoughts with the people who are important in your life, proceed to the map section that follows.

WHAT PART OF AMERICA IS RIGHT FOR YOU?

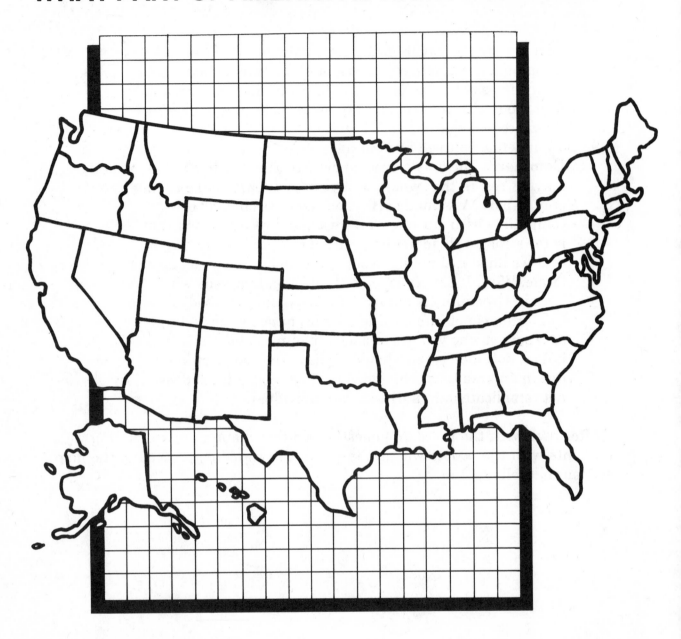

1. Do you want to live someplace else?

2. Where are the places you have considered living?

3. Do you wish to live in a different climate?

4. Have you traveled extensively to the places you are considering?

5. What are your major forms of recreation?

6. Where can you find challenging and rewarding work?

7. Are you limited financially to where you can live?

8. Is it important for you to live near relatives?

9. Are you limited where you can live by health?

10. **DO YOU REALLY WANT TO MOVE?**

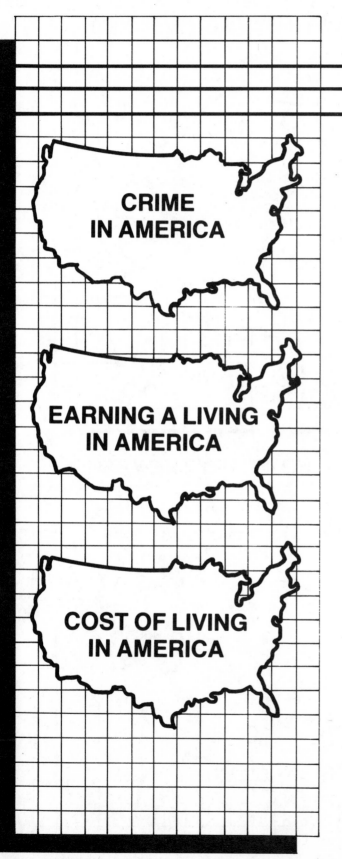

CRIME IN AMERICA

EARNING A LIVING IN AMERICA

COST OF LIVING IN AMERICA

BASED ON VIOLENT CRIME PER 100,000 INHABITANTS:

Safest States
1. North Dakota
2. South Dakota
3. New Hamphshire
4. Vermont
5. West Virginia

Most Dangerous States
1. Florida
2. New York
3. Maryland
4. California
5. Michigan

Source: 1985 Uniform Crime Reports, F.B.I.

THE TOP TEN HIGHEST AVERAGE SALARIED STATES:

1. Alaska $28,806
2. Washington D.C. $25,120
3. Michigan $20,940
4. New York $20,754
5. Connecticut $19,980
6. New Jersey $19,889
7. California $19,873
8. Illinois $19,733
9. Texas $18,864
10. Ohio $18,783

Source: Bureau of Labor Statistics, U.S. Labor Department, 1986

THE MOST EXPENSIVE AND LEAST EXPENSIVE STATES TO LIVE:
The Country's five wealthiest suburbs:*

1. Kenilworth, Illinois (Chicago)
2. Hunter's Creek, Texas (Houston)
3. Cherry Creek, Colorado (Denver)
4. Mission Hills, Kansas (Kansas City)
5. Piney Point, Texas (Houston)

Source: Roosevelt University Study

The Metro areas with the highest and lowest cost of living:**

Highest Costs
1. Stamford, Connecticut
2. Oxnard-Ventura, California
3. Norwalk, Connecticut
4. Honolulu, Hawaii
5. San Francisco, California

Lowest Costs
1. Joplin, Missouri
2. Anniston, Alabama
3. Gadsden, Alabama
4. Anderson, S. Carolina
5. Dothan, Alabama

Source: Rand McNally *Places Rated Almanac*

*Based on computer estimates of 1985 per capita income developed from 1983 census.

**Based on income required for homeownership, food and miscellaneous goods and services.

AMERICAN JOB GROWTH BY THE YEAR 2000

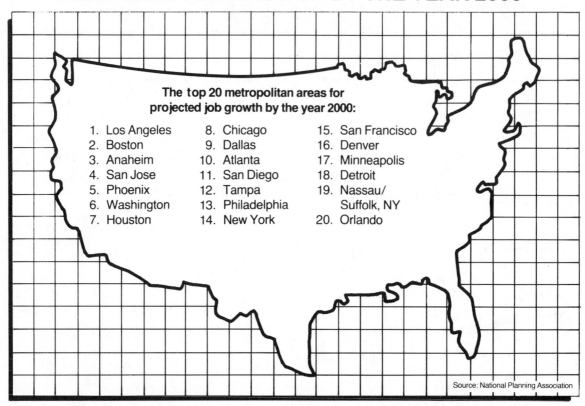

The top 20 metropolitan areas for projected job growth by the year 2000:

1. Los Angeles
2. Boston
3. Anaheim
4. San Jose
5. Phoenix
6. Washington
7. Houston
8. Chicago
9. Dallas
10. Atlanta
11. San Diego
12. Tampa
13. Philadelphia
14. New York
15. San Francisco
16. Denver
17. Minneapolis
18. Detroit
19. Nassau/ Suffolk, NY
20. Orlando

Source: National Planning Association

AMERICAN POPULATION GROWTH BY THE YEAR 2000

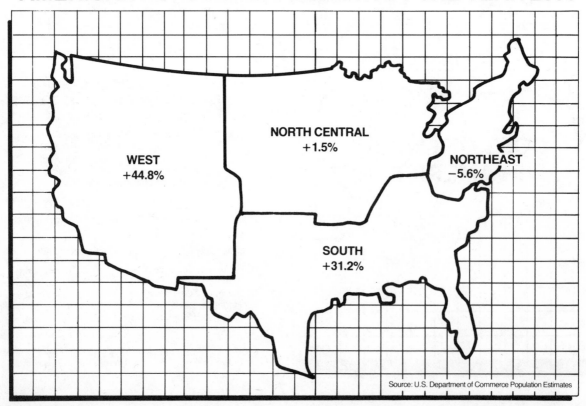

WEST
+44.8%

NORTH CENTRAL
+1.5%

NORTHEAST
−5.6%

SOUTH
+31.2%

Source: U.S. Department of Commerce Population Estimates

AMERICAN WEATHER

The numbers shown are based on the normal maximum temperatures for January and July by city, followed by the normal annual rainfall in inches.

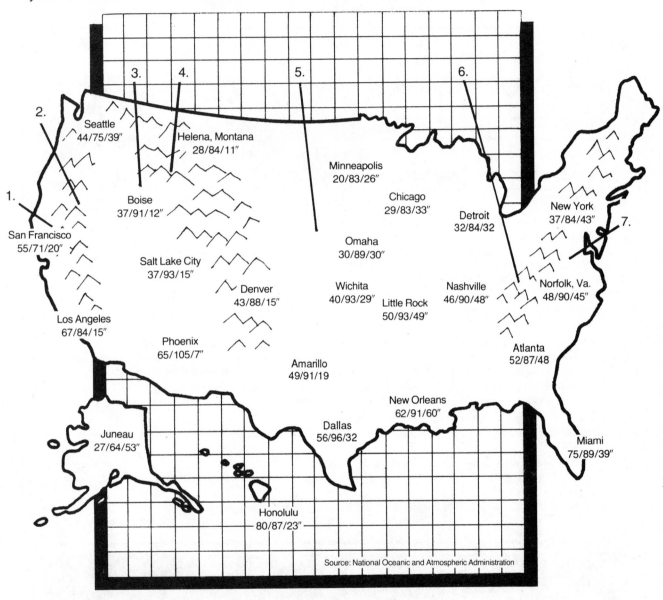

Seattle 44/75/39"
Helena, Montana 28/84/11"
Boise 37/91/12"
Salt Lake City 37/93/15"
Denver 43/88/15"
San Francisco 55/71/20"
Los Angeles 67/84/15"
Phoenix 65/105/7"
Amarillo 49/91/19
Juneau 27/64/53"
Honolulu 80/87/23"

Minneapolis 20/83/26"
Chicago 29/83/33"
Omaha 30/89/30"
Wichita 40/93/29"
Little Rock 50/93/49"
Dallas 56/96/32
New Orleans 62/91/60"

Detroit 32/84/32
Nashville 46/90/48"
Atlanta 52/87/48

New York 37/84/43"
Norfolk, Va. 48/90/45"
Miami 75/89/39"

Source: National Oceanic and Atmospheric Administration

The seven major climatic regions of the continental United States:

1. Pacific coast - mild.

2. Cascade-Sierra Nevada- cool summers, snowy winters.

3. Intermountain plateau - dry, semiarid.

4. Rocky mountain region - cool summers, snowy winters.

5. Great interior/southern plains/lowlands- weather extremes, hot summers, cold winters.

6. Appalachian mountain region - cool summers, snowy winters.

7. Middle/North Atlantic lowlands - milder winters, hot summers.

LIFEPLANNING LIBRARY GEOGRAPHY

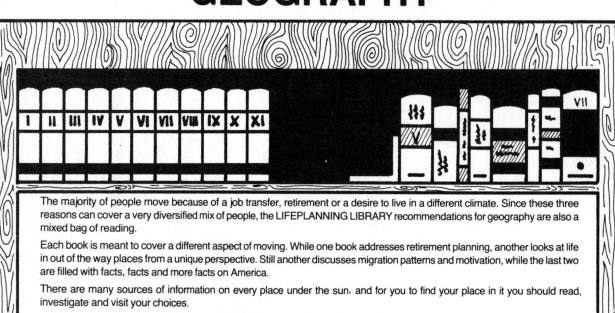

The majority of people move because of a job transfer, retirement or a desire to live in a different climate. Since these three reasons can cover a very diversified mix of people, the LIFEPLANNING LIBRARY recommendations for geography are also a mixed bag of reading.

Each book is meant to cover a different aspect of moving. While one book addresses retirement planning, another looks at life in out of the way places from a unique perspective. Still another discusses migration patterns and motivation, while the last two are filled with facts, facts and more facts on America.

There are many sources of information on every place under the sun, and for you to find your place in it you should read, investigate and visit your choices.

LIFEPLANNING LIBRARY RECOMMENDATIONS:

* *Places Rated Almanac* by Richard Boyer and David Savageau. Rand McNally & Company, NY (1985).
    — an excellent source of information on 329 U.S. metropolitan areas. Includes ranking and comparisons for climate, health, crime, housing, culture and cost of living. For retirement planning, they have *Places Rated Retirement Guide*.

* *Blue Highways* by William Least Heat Moon. Atlantic-Little, Brown Books, Boston/Toronto (1982).
    — a lovely look at America's out of the way locations and a roadmap to one man's struggle to rethink his priorities.

* *Encyclopedia Americana,* Grolier Incorporated, Danbury, Conn.
    — Between the 30 volumes and the index, you receive the basic information to get you started on exploring practically any location.

* *The New Heartland* by John Herbers, Times Books, NY (1986).
    — An interesting well written discussion of how migration patterns and motivations for moving have changed our national character.

* *Birnbaum's United States 1987* by Stephen Birnbaum. Houghton Mifflin Company, Boston (1986).
    — While this book is first and foremost a travel guide, it is full of information on American cities, resorts, regions and recreation areas.

PART THREE

LIFEPLANNING:
THE PHILOSOPHY

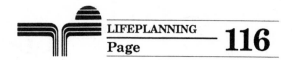

VIII. THE BALANCE

"Our aspirations are our possibilities."

Robert Browning

The message of this chapter is that we need to be successful in each of the key areas of living if we are to find a real and sustaining happiness.

For instance, tremendous wealth with few friends or family members would be an empty success. A wonderful career could be short lived without proper attention to one's health.

To ensure that a person is doing well in each of the key areas of life, *LIFEPLANNING* has established minimum levels to which your score should be compared. Any deficiencies you might have will become quickly apparent, and, in turn, you will be made aware of the importance of balance in life. This chapter is presented almost entirely in graphic form to help you better develop a visual picture of how you are doing in the key areas of life.

Up to this point, *LIFEPLANNING* has focused on stories of how others are doing, how you are doing as assessed in the tests, and how you can do better by living by the commandments. The next few pages focus on your scores in the five key areas of life. By filling out the charts with your scores, you will be able to

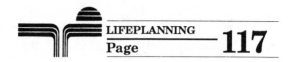

graphically depict where you are in need of fine-tuning or a concentrated effort to improve. To begin, fill in your score for each of the five individual charts.

LIFEPLANNING AREAS	YOUR TEST SCORES
Health*	_____
Wealth	_____
Recreation	_____
Career	_____
Companionship	_____
YOUR TOTAL *LIFEPLANNING* SCORE	_____

To determine your status within each **LIFEPLANNING** area, transfer your individual scores to the following pages. After completing each individual chart, plot all five of your scores on the **LIFEPLANNING** chart to see if you are maintaining balance among the five key areas of living.

* For purposes of developing a total LIFEPLANNING score, the maximum allowable score for Health is 155. If your Health score is higher, congratulations and keep up the good work. However, only record a score of 155 for this section.

HEALTH

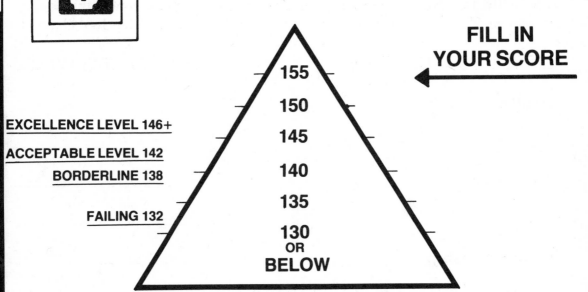

FILL IN YOUR SCORE ←

155
150
145
140
135
130
OR
BELOW

EXCELLENCE LEVEL 146+

ACCEPTABLE LEVEL 142

BORDERLINE 138

FAILING 132

Everyone that takes the health test starts with a score of 150 points and has an additional chance to earn 5 more points with the questions from the "Your Outlook" section. All the questions are based on medical, census and actuarial statistics and tables. While some elements of the test may seem out of your control, practically every situation has an action that you can take to counter a potentially negative impact. For instance, if your family health history has a strong reoccurrence of a particular health problem, your awareness and proper medical supervision can oftentimes keep the family health pattern from repeating or at least held to a minimum. The point is to take control of your own health destiny with professional medical help and personal attention. You can make a difference!

The bottom line on your health score is that you should not settle for a score of less than 150 points. If you are settling for less you should also be prepared to have your life end prematurely. Here are the steps you can take to help insure that you live your fair share:

●Fill out the above health chart with your test score.

●Determine your rank and how many points it will take to raise your score to the excellence level or higher.

●Review the health questions that cost you points and take the necessary actions to remedy your shortcomings (see chapter, The Beginning).

●Reread the commandments on good health.

WEALTH

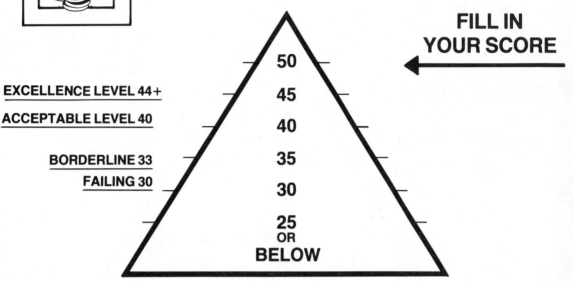

FILL IN
YOUR SCORE ←

EXCELLENCE LEVEL 44+

ACCEPTABLE LEVEL 40

BORDERLINE 33

FAILING 30

50
45
40
35
30
25
OR
BELOW

For the purpose of rating your financial wellness, the LIFEPLANNING test on wealth was designed with a scale of 1 to 50. A score of less than 40 points indicates a financial situation that needs some fixing. To make the test fair for people under 30, an acceptable level can be determined by adding ten years to your age and using that number as an intermediate target. This should be done with the understanding that 44 or higher is the ongoing goal everyone should work towards.

Do not be discouraged if your financial score is coming up short. The test is designed to compare your financial habits, knowledge and profile against an exacting standard. Money is cited over and over again as a major contributor to divorce and discord in relationships when it is not handled properly or is in too short of supply. It is important that you raise your financial score and handle your money properly if you are going to keep money from being a problem. Here are the steps you can take to help insure your financial wellness:

- Fill out the above wealth chart with your test score.

- Determine your rank and how many points it will take to raise your score to the excellence level or higher.

- Review the wealth questions that cost you points and take the necessary actions to remedy your shortcomings (see chapter, The Beginning).

- Reread the commandments on financial wellness.

RECREATION

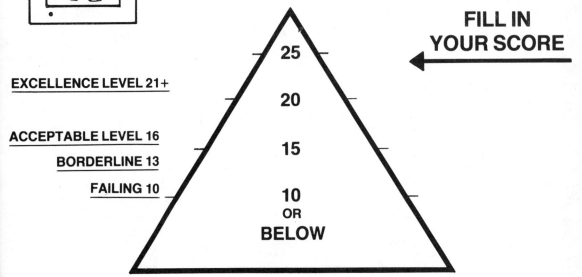

FILL IN
YOUR SCORE

25

20

15

10
OR
BELOW

EXCELLENCE LEVEL 21+

ACCEPTABLE LEVEL 16

BORDERLINE 13

FAILING 10

How are you doing in the area of recreation? Are you leading an active, diversified life filled with a variety of social, cultural, intellectual and athletic pastimes? If your score is below 16, the answer is no. People that have an active life filled with a quality balance of pursuits will typically score well above 16. Those below 16 have allowed their life to get out of balance and are cheating themselves out of a special part of living.

Recreational pursuits are important because they provide us both physical and mental exercise. They serve as a reward after work. They help us achieve a special mood that lets us blow off steam or forget our responsibilities for the moment. They promote important self-growth. To help you develop and maintain a personal program of recreation, please review the following:

- Fill out the above recreation chart with your test score.

- Determine your rank and how many points it will take to raise your score to the excellence level or higher.

- Review the recreation questions that cost you points and take the necessary actions to remedy your shortcomings (see chapter, The Beginning).

- Reread the commandments on recreation.

COMPANIONSHIP

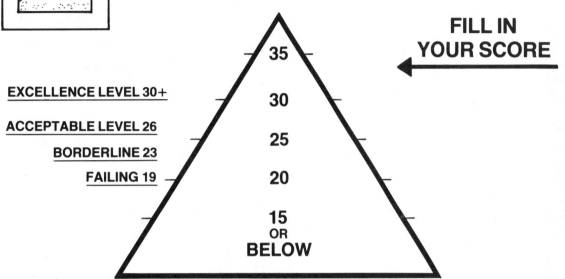

35

30

25

20

15
OR
BELOW

**FILL IN
YOUR SCORE** ⟵

EXCELLENCE LEVEL 30+

ACCEPTABLE LEVEL 26

BORDERLINE 23

FAILING 19

Are you less than perfect as a companion? Probably no matter what our score, we could all use some improvement in this area. For the sake of improvement, it is important to use a numerical scale and a score of less than 26 signals potential trouble. A score of 23 or less places too much of a burden on your friends and 19 or less means you are risking any relationships you have left.

How we treat others, see ourselves and approach the world in fact defines our world. The ultimate importance we place on friendship and relationships will vary from person to person but the ultimate need for companionship in some form is universal. To help you both give and receive friendship and love, please go through the following steps:

- •Fill out the above companionship chart with your test score.

- •Determine your rank and how many points it will take to raise your score to the excellence level or higher.

- •Review the companionship questions that cost you points and take the necessary actions to remedy your shortcomings (see chapter, The Beginning).

- •Reread the commandments on companionship.

CAREER

FILL IN
YOUR SCORE ←

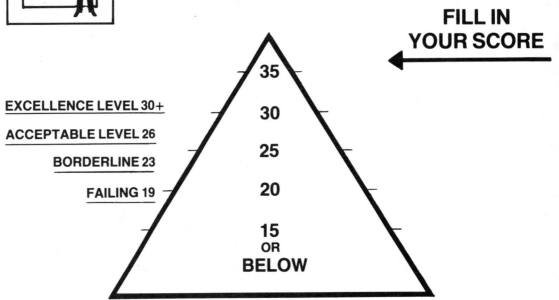

EXCELLENCE LEVEL 30+

ACCEPTABLE LEVEL 26

BORDERLINE 23

FAILING 19

35

30

25

20

15
OR
BELOW

Ranking how you are doing in your career is done on a scale of 1 to 35. A score of less than 19 means serious trouble in the workplace. Scoring that low indicates you are ill-suited for your work or not fitting into your work environment. Either way, those types of problems must be faced or you must be prepared to face failure. A score of 23 is a little better but still not good enough. A score of 26 is acceptable and 30 or higher is the range we should all strive for in our work.

In the chapter on careers, considerable time is spent pointing out the tremendous amount of time we spend at our work. In addition to the many hours we devote to our work, most of us feel that our work is a very important part of us. This time, energy and part of ourselves that we put into our work is so important in fact, that we owe it to ourselves to make sure we are matched up with work that is right for us. Review the following steps to insure that you are on the right career path:

●Fill out the above career chart with your test score.

●Determine your rank and how many points it will take to raise your score to the excellence level or higher.

●Review the career questions that cost you points and take the necessary actions to remedy your shortcomings (see chapter, The Beginning).
●Reread the commandments on career.

CHART YOUR LIFE BALANCE

PLOT YOUR SCORES ON THE BALANCE CHART

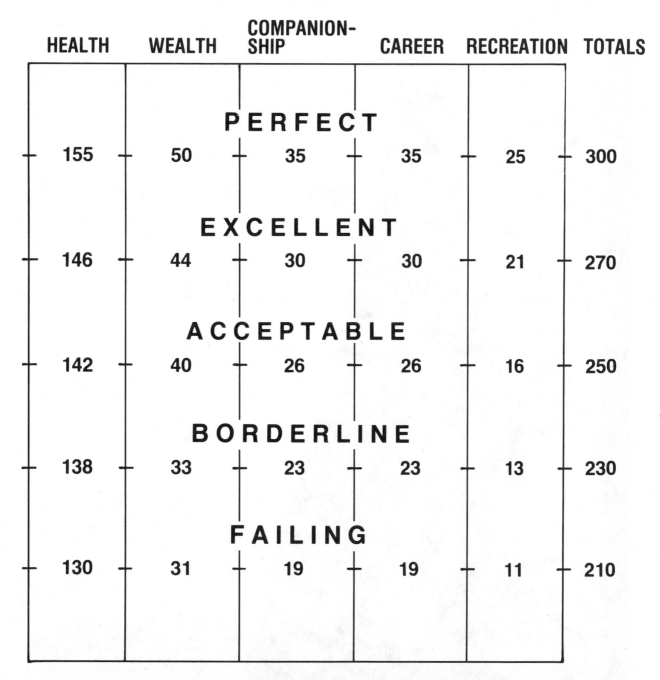

HEALTH	WEALTH	COMPANION-SHIP	CAREER	RECREATION	TOTALS
		P E R F E C T			
155	50	35	35	25	300
		E X C E L L E N T			
146	44	30	30	21	270
		A C C E P T A B L E			
142	40	26	26	16	250
		B O R D E R L I N E			
138	33	23	23	13	230
		F A I L I N G			
130	31	19	19	11	210

A central message of LIFEPLANNING is the importance of balance between the five key areas of life. To find a real and lasting happiness in life we must find, nurture and preserve success in health, wealth, companionship, career and recreation.

If you plot your various LIFEPLANNING scores on the above chart, you will see if your life is in balance. Ideally, you will have close to a straight line going across the chart and that line will be in the excellence range or above. Areas of your life in need of work should be clear to you and the preceding charts in this chapter should have you well on your way to addressing any shortcomings.

The next page shows you graphically how you are doing overall in life. The next chapter provides you with the tools to begin the daily process of improving your life.

THE ROAD OF LIFEPLANNING

**Here is an opportunity to see how you are doing overall in life.
Take your LIFEPLANNING cumulative scores for the five tests
and see where you are on the road of LIFEPLANNING:**

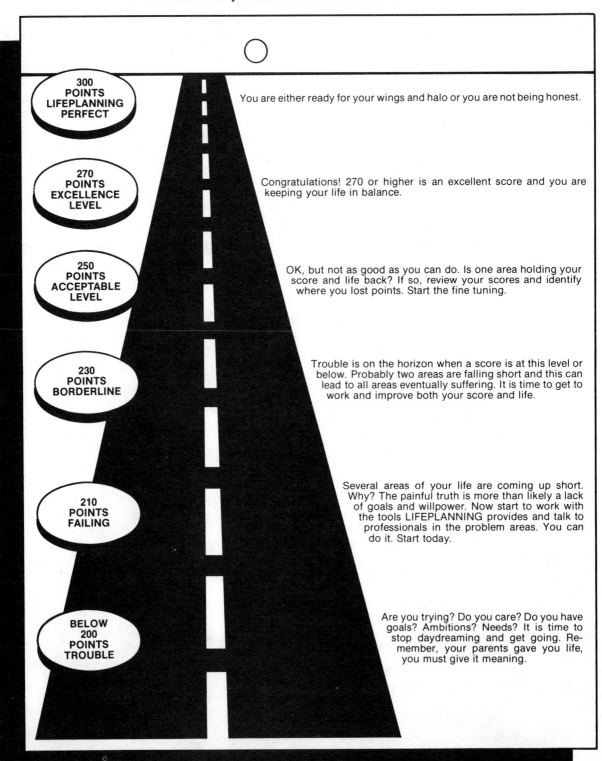

300 POINTS LIFEPLANNING PERFECT

You are either ready for your wings and halo or you are not being honest.

270 POINTS EXCELLENCE LEVEL

Congratulations! 270 or higher is an excellent score and you are keeping your life in balance.

250 POINTS ACCEPTABLE LEVEL

OK, but not as good as you can do. Is one area holding your score and life back? If so, review your scores and identify where you lost points. Start the fine tuning.

230 POINTS BORDERLINE

Trouble is on the horizon when a score is at this level or below. Probably two areas are falling short and this can lead to all areas eventually suffering. It is time to get to work and improve both your score and life.

210 POINTS FAILING

Several areas of your life are coming up short. Why? The painful truth is more than likely a lack of goals and willpower. Now start to work with the tools LIFEPLANNING provides and talk to professionals in the problem areas. You can do it. Start today.

BELOW 200 POINTS TROUBLE

Are you trying? Do you care? Do you have goals? Ambitions? Needs? It is time to stop daydreaming and get going. Remember, your parents gave you life, you must give it meaning.

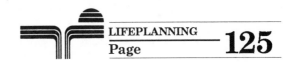

CHAPTER NINE

LIFEPLANNING:
THE BEGINNING

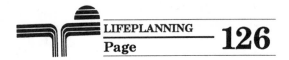

IX. THE BEGINNING

"Nothing in the world can take the place of persistence. Talent will not;
nothing is more common than unsuccessful men with talent. Genius will not;
the world is full of educated derelicts. Persistence and determination alone
are omnipotent. The slogan 'press on' has solved and always will solve the
problems of the human race."

Calvin Coolidge

This chapter provides the organizational materials you need to keep a diary on
your progress while earning the points missed on the *LIFEPLANNING* tests.
More importantly, the diary approach will assist you in improving your life. But
you must provide the motivation to both keep the diary and change your life.

That you have gotten this far is an excellent indication you are concerned about
the quality of your life and how to improve it. All you need to do now is take what
you have learned from the tests and apply it to day-to-day living.

Sound simple? Maybe too simple? Just take what you have learned and apply
it? How can that possibly work? Don't you have to start a fad diet? Send money
to a faithhealer? Believe in a magical cure? Live by some quirky rules?

No. No again. A thousand times no!

Success in life does not come from "here today, gone tomorrow" cures. Success

comes from earning your money honestly and investing it wisely. Success comes to you by living according to the statistical percentages established by the finest medical, financial, and professional minds in the world. Success comes to you through intelligent, motivated planning for life and hard work.

In the opening pages of this book, we promised no miracle cures or magic potions for health, wealth, or happiness. We made it clear that to get ahead, you needed to apply hard work, common sense, intelligence, and discipline to a well-defined set of goals. Throughout these pages, you have been given the opportunity to develop those goals. In this chapter, you will be able to write them down and develop a step-by-step approach to achieving each and every one of your aspirations. No miracles, magic, fads, or short-cuts. Just common sense.

Two final points need to be made before you go on to developing your own goal-achievement diary. The first concerns luck. The day you picked up this copy of *LIFEPLANNING*, yours changed. No longer is good luck something that may or may not be with you. Now you will make your own good fortune. Does this mean that nothing bad will come your way? Of course not, but it means that if you put into place the positive, confident attitude started by the daily practice of *LIFEPLANNING*, you will create opportunities to prosper and win. Chances for success will be more forthcoming, and you will be able to more readily identify and capitalize on them.

The final point concerns attitude. The importance of a positive attitude toward life is mentioned repeatedly throughout these pages, but unlike some books, *LIFEPLANNING* believes that to reach success, we must combine a positive attitude with education, discipline, and hard work. Be wary of prophets who preach the power of a positive attitude but fail to mention these other essential elements. What they are selling will be hard to resist until you realize that it is worthless. Too often, that realization comes only after you have invested your money, time, and hope.

As an example, some proponents of the power of positive thinking advocate that by believing enough in something, you will make it so. Not true. As an example, thinking thin is not enough. You also must eat less and exercise more, and anyone who tells you differently is being unfair and dishonest with you.

Always believe you can attain your goals, but complement that attitude with the clearly defined steps and discipline that will take you there.

Let's get started on those goals by first studying some examples of others on their road to self-improvement through *LIFEPLANNING*.

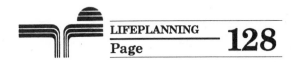

GOAL ACHIEVEMENT DIARY - SAMPLE ONE

Person: Allen H.   Age: 45   Occupation: Attorney
Marital Status: Married

Allen's scoring on the *LIFEPLANNING* tests was strong in all but one area - health. As a married father of two with a thriving law practice and an active social life, he brought considerable organizational skills to his career and asset building, as well as admirable success in the area of companionship. He fell down in the area of health, though, and you will see that those shortcomings also hurt his score in recreation.

Allen's *LIFEPLANNING* profile, problems, and **LIFEPLAN** follow.

LIFEPLANNING PROFILE

LIFEPLANNING AREA	ALLEN'S SCORE	BORDERLINE/ EXCELLENT	ALLEN'S GOAL
Health	123	138/146	23 points
Wealth	42	33/44	Fine-tuning
Recreation	15	13/21	6 points
Career	28	23/30	Ongoing commitment
Companionship	31	23/30	Fine-tuning

LIFEPLANNING PROBLEMS

Allen's specific problems in the area of health that cost him points were:

Management position	4 points
Type A personality	6 points
City dweller	4 points
Office job	4 points
Smoker	12 points
Medical checkup	2 points
Medical awareness	1 point
Regular aerobic exercise	6 points
Overweight {12 lbs.}	3 points
Sexual Activity	1 point

LIFEPLAN

For Allen to improve his score and his health to the acceptable level, he needs to gain 19 points. To move up to the excellence level, he needs 23 points.

His management position, office job, and home in the city were conscious choices, and while statistically they can have a negative health impact, he did not want to make any changes in those areas. Changing a type A personality is, according to some doctors, very difficult, if not impossible. While Allen should make a concerted effort to slow down and reduce stress, it would be unrealistic to eliminate or add points for modifying this personality trait.

The good news is that the remaining areas provide ample opportunity for Allen to alter his lifestyle and earn the needed points to bring his health approach back in line with accepted medical practice. By quitting smoking, going in for regular checkups, losing weight, and exercising, he could bring his score and health into the excellence range.

In Allen's case, he decided to quit smoking with the help of the American Cancer Society. He has not stopped entirely, but he is cutting back, and his family is being very supportive. His diet started after a complete medical exam and continued with the help of a weight-loss center recommended by his doctor. The exercise program is evolving slowly after considerable experimentation. He has tried swimming, walking, running, cycling, and various combinations. He is trying to find exercise that provides him aerobic workouts as well as enjoyment.

LIFEPLANNING PROGNOSIS

Allen will achieve his health goals through his efforts, the support of his family, and guidance from professionals. It will not come overnight, but his persistence will ensure that he has many more nights and days in his life to enjoy due to improved health.

GOAL ACHIEVEMENT DIARY - SAMPLE TWO

Persons: Joe and Sandy A.   Ages: 32 and 29
Occupations: Salesman and Graphic Illustrator
Marital Status: Married, one child, six years old.

Joe and Sandy were a popular couple. Both were outgoing, fun to be with, and they filled their lives with all the adult toys. A hot tub, motorboat, large screen television, two sports cars, and a great condo made them both the life and center of a lot of parties. Friends were always stopping by for a drink, a swim, or a boat ride. When they took the *LIFEPLANNING* tests one night along with some other friends, it was on a lark. Just another excuse to get together and party.

The results were sobering. In companionship, career, and health, their scores were acceptable. In recreation, as expected, they scored high. In wealth, the results were a disaster. Here are their *LIFEPLANNING* profiles, problems, and **LIFEPLAN**.

LIFEPLANNING PROFILE

LIFEPLANNING AREA	JOE'S SCORE/ SANDY'S SCORE	EXCELLENT LEVEL	JOE'S GOAL/ SANDY'S GOAL
Health	144/147	146	Ongoing commitment
Wealth	Combined: 14	44	30 points
Recreation	18/19	21	Fine-tuning
Career	27/25	30	3 points/5 points
Companionship	28/28	30	Fine-tuning

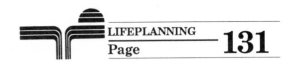

LIFEPLANNING PROBLEMS

While every area of their lives could stand some improvement, Joe's and Sandy's financial situation was a disaster waiting to happen. The litany of their financial pitfalls was long:

No will	1 point
No IRA or pension plan	1 point
Not current on credit cards	1 point
No idea how much they owed	1 point
No budget	1 point
Five incorrect financial answers	5 points
Inadequate emergency savings	4 points
Too much installment debt	4 points
Not enough annual savings	4 points
Too little net worth	4 points

To improve their situation, Joe and Sandy needed to focus on their finances before they had a negative impact on every other aspect of their lives. Their score placed them in a failing category, and they faced financial doom if any interruption stopped their incomes. They were still paying all their bills, but only because Joe was bringing in some big commission checks. Any downturn in his sales performance, and they would not be able to meet their monthly obligations.

They had taken no steps to plan for retirement or the future, including their son's college education, only 12 years away. They also failed to protect his future by drawing up a will. If anything were to happen to them, they assumed their son would get everything, and that a family member would take care of him. Because of their lack of financial knowledge, they did not know their assets could be kept from him for a prolonged time if they died intestate. Also, while Sandy assumed her sister would take the boy, Joe had never given it any thought. This could leave their son in a legal limbo, all for the want of a simple will.

The problems continued with inadequate emergency savings, no long-term savings account, and no attempt at financial planning with a budget.

LIFEPLAN

Joe's and Sandy's serious shortcomings in the financial area call for them to get professional guidance from a qualified financial expert.

To get started on a financial plan, they must stop buying on installment until they get their consumer debt below 12 percent of their take-home pay.

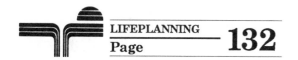

First and foremost, this means stopping credit purchases and setting a percentage of their paychecks aside each pay period. Ideally, payroll deductions would be best for these two to help force savings. Developing a will, an IRA account, and college fund for their son also are top priorities. They might have to sell an asset like the motorboat or snowmobile or cut back on their socializing. Joe and Sandy are literally hocking their future with excessive spending today.

LIFEPLANNING PROGNOSIS

In Joe and Sandy's case, the future was not bright. Their inability to manage money and their lack of discipline in consumer spending would eventually create some financial hardships when Sandy loses her job. Over and over again, money is listed as one of the greatest problems in relationships, and the problem proved to be too great for Sandy and Joe. They eventually divorced.

GOAL ACHIEVEMENT DIARY - SAMPLE THREE

Person: R.E.   Age: 29   Occupation: Marketing Executive

Marital Status: Married

R. E. 's scoring on the *LIFEPLANNING* tests were a disappointment in every category except career. As a young man, he had already earned a tremendous amount of money in commissions, salary and bonuses. Additionally, he had been promoted almost on a yearly basis. His life was classically tilted towards work and away from all the other key areas of living.

R.E.'s *LIFEPLANNING* profile, problems and **LIFEPLAN** follow.

LIFEPLANNING PROFILE

LIFEPLANNING AREA	R.E.'S SCORE	BORDERLINE/ EXCELLENT	R.E.'s GOAL
Health	103	138/146	43 points
Wealth	25	33/44	19 points
Recreation	10	13/21	11 points
Career	35	23/30	Too high?
Companionship	18	23/30	12 points

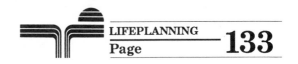

LIFEPLANNING PROBLEMS

R. E.'s specific problems were many. Here's a partial list of the areas costing him points:

HEALTH
Type A personality
Family history of health problems
Heavy smoker and drinker
No medical checkups or awareness
No exercise
Overweight
Workaholic
> Total Health Score: 103 points

WEALTH
No will
No IRA
No savings
No budget
Too much installment debt
To little net worth
> Total Wealth Score: 25

CAREER
Perfect score

RECREATION AND COMPANIONSHIP
Workaholic tendencies
No exercise or significant cultural interests
No involvement in community life
> Total Recreation Score: 10
> Total Companionship Score: 18

LIFEPLAN

R.E. was the classic workaholic. His total preoccupation with his career and acquiring material possessions left little time for, nor interest in, recreation, civic involvement or companionship. He certainly was not a bad person, just someone who had allowed his life to get completely out of balance. To get his life back on track, he had to start with health, eliminating smoking and excessive drinking, and getting a check-up. He also was in need of a diet and exercise plan. In the area of wealth, he needed to budget, save, and plan. In

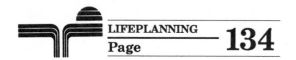
recreation and companionship, he needed friends and interests outside of his workplace. Additionally, he needed to shift the constant focus off himself and develop an interest in others.

LIFEPLANNING PROGNOSIS

R.E. achieved his goals in the areas of health (raising his score by 50 points), wealth (raising his score by 16 points), companionship (raising his score by 8 points), and recreation (doubling his score). To accomplish that gain of more than 80 points, he needed to control his workaholic tendencies and, understandably, his career score dropped a few points.

What at first seemed like drudgery for R.E. eventually became a great source of pleasure.

Quitting smoking made him feel better. Life without hangovers was more pleasant. Weight loss and exercise complemented each other and increased his energy level.

He surprised himself with the discovery that better money management meant he required less income. He stopped defining himelf by his possessions and bought only what he needed. He began to look at owning a business and leaving the corporate world behind.

In recreation, he rediscovered reading, theater, museums, and traveling. In companionship, he found out that work associates, while they are important, cannot take the place of family and intimate friendships.

Make no mistake about it. R.E., through *LIFEPLANNING*, did not discover paradise. Instead, he rediscovered that work, while important, only partly defines the person. That companionship and recreation are the roses that everyone must stop to smell. That possessions sometimes own the person instead of the other way around.

He also found out that education and discovery should never stop for individuals who want to continue to grow and prosper.

The following pages are filled with several blank goal achievement diaries. Fill out the scoring information at the top of each calendar, and then write your *LIFEPLANNING* profile, problems, goals, and **LIFEPLAN** in the appropriate blanks. After filling in all the necessary information, use the calendar to keep track of your progress.

Here's an important tip: Fill out the calendar in advance with your plans to achieve your goals. Then fill out how you are doing on a daily basis. Good luck, and do not delay!

TOTAL ACHIEVEMENT DIARY

Name: _____

LIFEPLANNING SCORES

	Your Score		Excellent Score		Points Needed
Health	_____	Vs.	146	=	_____
Wealth	_____	Vs.	44	=	_____
Recreation	_____	Vs	21	=	_____
Companionship	_____	Vs.	30	=	_____
Career	_____	Vs.	30	=	_____

LIFEPLANNING PROBLEMS

_____

_____

LIFE PLAN

_____

_____

_____

_____

LIFEPLANNING

To keep your LIFEPLAN within reach, chart out your goals for the next two weeks, i.e., start a budget, get a will, start a diet and exercise program, write a letter, see a play, etc. Write the specific events or actions down in advance and record how you actually do. Record your progress and KEEP TRACK OF YOUR POINT GAINS (AND LOSSES). START TODAY!

	Sunday	Monday	Tuesday	Wednesday	Thursday	Friday	Saturday
GOALS Week One							
ACTION Week One							
GOALS WEEK TWO							
ACTION Week Two							

PROGRESS

TOTAL ACHIEVEMENT DIARY

Name: _____

LIFEPLANNING SCORES

	Your Score		Excellent Score		Points Needed
Health	_____	Vs.	146	=	_____
Wealth	_____	Vs.	44	=	_____
Recreation	_____	Vs	21	=	_____
Companionship	_____	Vs.	30	=	_____
Career	_____	Vs.	30	=	_____

LIFEPLANNING PROBLEMS

_____

_____

_____

LIFE PLAN

_____

_____

_____

_____

_____

LIFEPLANNING

To keep your LIFEPLAN within reach, chart out your goals for the next two weeks, i.e., start a budget, get a will, start a diet and exercise program, write a letter, see a play, etc. Write the specific events or actions down in advance and record how you actually do. Record your progress and KEEP TRACK OF YOUR POINT GAINS (AND LOSSES). START TODAY!

	Sunday	Monday	Tuesday	Wednesday	Thursday	Friday	Saturday
GOALS Week One							
ACTION Week One							
GOALS WEEK TWO							
ACTION Week Two							

PROGRESS

TOTAL ACHIEVEMENT DIARY

Name: _____

LIFEPLANNING SCORES

	Your Score		Excellent Score		Points Needed
Health	_____	Vs.	146	=	_____
Wealth	_____	Vs.	44	=	_____
Recreation	_____	Vs	21	=	_____
Companionship	_____	Vs.	30	=	_____
Career	_____	Vs.	30	=	_____

LIFEPLANNING PROBLEMS

_____

_____

LIFE PLAN

_____

_____

_____

_____

_____

LIFEPLANNING

To keep your LIFEPLAN within reach, chart out your goals for the next two weeks, i.e., start a budget, get a will, start a diet and exercise program, write a letter, see a play, etc. Write the specific events or actions down in advance and record how you actually do. Record your progress and KEEP TRACK OF YOUR POINT GAINS (AND LOSSES). START TODAY!

	Sunday	Monday	Tuesday	Wednesday	Thursday	Friday	Saturday
GOALS Week One							
ACTION Week One							
GOALS WEEK TWO							
ACTION Week Two							

PROGRESS

LIFEPLANNING

To keep your LIFEPLAN within reach, chart out your goals for the next two weeks, i.e., start a budget, get a will, start a diet and exercise program, write a letter, see a play, etc. Write the specific events or actions down in advance and record how you actually do. Record your progress and KEEP TRACK OF YOUR POINT GAINS (AND LOSSES). START TODAY!

	Sunday	Monday	Tuesday	Wednesday	Thursday	Friday	Saturday
GOALS Week One							
ACTION Week One							
GOALS WEEK TWO							
ACTION Week Two							

PROGRESS _____

LIFEPLANNING

To keep your LIFEPLAN within reach, chart out your goals for the next two weeks, i.e., start a budget, get a will, start a diet and exercise program, write a letter, see a play, etc. Write the specific events or actions down in advance and record how you actually do. Record your progress and KEEP TRACK OF YOUR POINT GAINS (AND LOSSES). START TODAY!

	Sunday	Monday	Tuesday	Wednesday	Thursday	Friday	Saturday
GOALS Week One							
ACTION Week One							
GOALS WEEK TWO							
ACTION Week Two							

PROGRESS _____

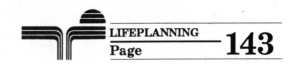

CHAPTER TEN

LIFEPLANNING:
THE BELIEF

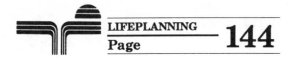

THE BELIEF

"For what shall it profit a man, if he gain the
whole world and lose his own soul?"

Book of Mark (8:36)
New Testament

If these few final words of **LIFEPLANNING** could be shouted from the rooftops or preached from the pulpit, they would be. Every page, every chart, every question, and every answer in this book is dedicated to the principle that you are important, special, and unique in all the world.

The central belief of **LIFEPLANNING** is that individuals have the ultimate control and sole responsibility for their future. Granted, factors out of every individual's control will come into play and influence one's life, but **LIFEPLANNING** realizes that only the factors within our own control can be changed by us and asks that we focus our attention and energy on those variables.

One of the most beautiful experiences we can have is the mastery, if even for a moment, over a piece of our destiny. Guiding ourselves successfully through an endeavor that contributes and adds to our own well-being triggers a fundamental emotion within us that stands shoulder to shoulder with all other positive

feelings save one. And that one brings us to the final message of *LIFEPLANNING*.

Only one other experience surpasses guiding our own future, and that is contributing to the future of someone else. Those who do not know this and have not felt it are missing an essential part of life. *LIFEPLANNING* was built upon a foundation of how best to help others help themselves, and this is as important a message as any contained within these pages. It transcends words and becomes an attitude, a spirit, a belief: a belief that life has meaning, purpose, and importance both for the individual and beyond the individual. To truly succeed, we must be selfish enough to help ourselves and selfless enough to help others.

Make no mistake, this is not a discussion of the personal God of Western religion or the mysticism of the religions of the Far East. In this chapter, we are not looking for rules or tests on living but, instead, reason and purpose for life itself.

The message is simple, not sophomoric. We live as a community or we risk life entirely. The wisdom is best captured in the *New Testament* in the book of Mark (8:36): "For what shall it profit a man, if he gain the whole world, and lose his own soul?"

LIFEPLANNING concludes on this important, albeit brief, message of community, because for us to best help others, we must ensure that we are doing all that we can to fulfill our potential. This is the balance of life: helping others while working toward our own success.

The controversial writer and philosopher Ayn Rand, in a collection of essays titled *The Virtue of Selfishness*, proposed that man must address a new morality known as objectivism. She believed rational self-interest taken to the extreme of rational selfishness and at the expense of altruism was necessary for personal survival and the survival of a free society.

In stark contrast to this radical theory of the importance of the individual stands Karl Marx's teachings of socialism. Marx believed that the individual must be secondary to the welfare of the masses. That government must control all.

In America, practically everyone falls somewhere in between the extremes of Ayn Rand and Karl Marx. Our democratic form of government is certainly the best in the world for creating an environment where the individual and the masses not only survive but thrive. Of course, any form of government is only as good as the individuals who comprise it. And as individuals, you must take responsibility for your success through disciplined and directed energy toward your goals, never forgetting to help others along the way.

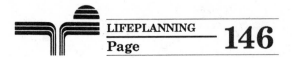

Robert Hutchins, a former president of the University of Chicago, said it best when describing his institution of higher learning: "The university isn't a very good school - it's just the best there is."

Each of us must struggle to honestly and humbly apply this to our lives. We must attempt to be the best we can be by working to control our own destiny and by contributing to the destiny of those around us. We must unleash this power within ourselves to realize our potential, and then go on to help others do the same. We must remember that obtaining our personal goals of excellence developed through the *LIFEPLANNING* tests, examples, and commandments, coupled with our own determination, will make our dreams achievable.

We must never give up. If at times we feel we are coming up short, we should remember the words of a woman who had so little to live for, Helen Keller. On the subject of persevering, Keller said, "Be of good cheer. Do not think of today's failures, but of the success that may come tomorrow.

"You have set yourselves a difficult task, but you will succeed if you persevere. And you will find a joy in overcoming obstacles. Remember, no effort made to attain something beautiful is ever lost."

Finally, we must realize the immensity of the universe and respect it. We must accept God and be the richer for it. We must keep ourselves surrounded by people whom we love and work that gives us satisfaction. We must be generous in our prosperity. We must treat our world with respect and approach it with enthusiasm. We must realize that life is filled with adversity and persevere. We must read good books, engage in meaningful conversations, go for long walks. We must understand the world as it is, but never stop in our personal efforts to make it better.

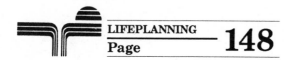
ABOUT THE ARTISTS

The watercolor on the previous page is an original work commissioned for *LIFEPLANNING* by noted artist James Metcalf. Mr. Metcalf's work has been shared with the public through gallery showings, books, and magazines, including *Arizona Highways*.

The illustrations, graphic designs, and cover artwork were done for *LIFEPLANNING* by Judith Coast. Ms. Coast's work was done while she was operating Judith Coast Graphic Designs. Currently, Ms. Coast is an artist for *The Arizona Republic*.

ABOUT THE AUTHOR

ROBB E. DALTON's intense curiosity about life found its first formal outlet at the age of 14 when he began working as a radio reporter and announcer. That led to his writing a weekly newspaper column at age 15. At 17, he was enrolling in university journalism classes.

Two years later, Robb's life was turned upside down when his father, at only age 42, died of a massive heart attack.

By working part-time, Robb was able to finish college, graduating first in his class at Wayne State College with a Summa Cum Laude degree in Communications. After moving through the ranks in advertising and broadcasting, Robb became the youngest president of a television group in America when, at only age 30, he was promoted to President and General Manager of the Kakeland Television Stations. Under his leadership, the stations won many national television awards, including the 1986 regional selection as one of the Edward R. Murrow "Television Stations of the Year."

Robb personally was honored for civic and station work, including his selection as "Outstanding Young Person of the Year" by the Jaycees in 1985.

Today, Robb pours his energy into researching and reporting the important principles of *LIFEPLANNING*. His *LIFEPLANNING* score is 271.

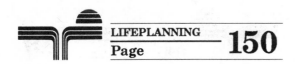

THE LIFEPLANNING COMMANDMENTS

FOR GOOD HEALTH

I.	Thou shall not smoke
II.	Thou shall eat a well-balanced, low-fat, high-fiber, nutritional diet
III.	Thou shall drink six glasses of water each day
IV.	Thou shall maintain the proper weight for your height and frame size
V.	Thou shall drink alcohol in moderation
VI.	Thou shall adhere to a set routine of aerobic exercise
VII.	Thou shall take a daily multiple vitamin containing the recommended dietary allowances
VIII.	Thou shall reduce stress
IX.	Thou shall have regular medical and dental checkups
X.	Thou shall reduce thy vulnerability to accidents

FOR FINANCIAL WELLNESS

I.	Thou shall have a properly executed will
II.	Thou shall develop a friendly, professional relationship with a banker
III.	Thou shall buy a home
IV.	Thou shall maintain an excellent credit rating
V.	Thou shall develop and adhere to a personal budget
VI.	Thou shall have adequate insurance
VII.	Thou shall plan, prepare, and save for retirement
VIII.	Thou shall develop a savings plan
IX.	Thou shall be a comparison shopper
X.	Thou shall not define thyself by thy possessions

FOR INTELLECTUAL, CULTURAL, AND PHYSICAL FITNESS

I.	Thou shall limit passive participation
II.	Thou shall become active in an organization or club
III.	Thou shall keep thy personal life distinct from thy professional life
IV.	Thou shall have a diversified program of intellectual recreation
V.	Thou shall never stop growing intellectually fit
VI.	Thou shall adhere to a set routine of aerobic exercise
VII.	Thou shall develop a lifetime approach to sports and fitness
VIII.	Thou shall maintain a complete but calm approach to competition
IX.	Thou shall seek proper instruction and teaching
X.	Thou shall not bore others with intellectual or athletic achievements

FOR CAREER SATISFACTION

I.	Thou shall spend thy career doing what thy enjoys and does well
II.	Thou shall insist on gaining, maintaining, and increasing the knowledge needed in thy work
III.	Thou shall understand thy strengths
IV.	Thou shall know thy weaknesses
V.	Thou shall understand thy company's politics and not play them
VI.	Thou shall develop listening skills
VII.	Thou shall trust thy instincts
VIII.	Thou shall not procrastinate
IX.	Thou shall have both short- and long-term goals
X.	Thou shall enjoy as thy go

FOR COMPANIONSHIP

I.	Thou shall be a good listener
II.	Thou shall give criticism in a positive, nurturing manner
III.	Thou shall accept criticism with an open mind
IV.	Thou shall remember the little things
V.	Thou shall hug, cuddle, and comfort
VI.	Thou shall share the positives and the negatives
VII.	Thou shall work to always look thy best
VIII.	Thou shall have realistic expectations in thy relationships
IX.	Thou shall seek intimate friendships as well as professional friendships
X.	Thou shall give everything, and then give a little more

INDEX

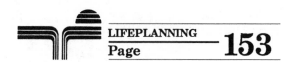

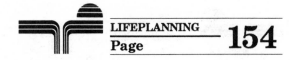

LIFEPLANNING MAKES THE PERFECT GIFT!

If you would like to help a friend, family member or co-worker improve the quality of their life send them a copy of **LIFEPLANNING**. It is the ideal Birthday, Christmas or Graduation present and a simple, inexpensive way to tell someone you are interested in their success.

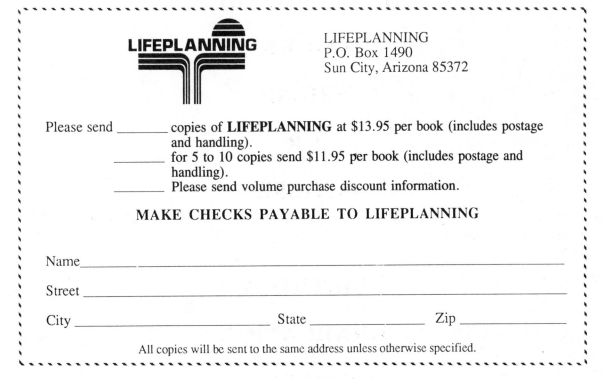

LIFEPLANNING
P.O. Box 1490
Sun City, Arizona 85372

Please send _____ copies of **LIFEPLANNING** at $13.95 per book (includes postage and handling).

_____ for 5 to 10 copies send $11.95 per book (includes postage and handling).

_____ Please send volume purchase discount information.

MAKE CHECKS PAYABLE TO LIFEPLANNING

Name_____

Street _____

City _____ State _____ Zip _____

All copies will be sent to the same address unless otherwise specified.

LIFEPLANNING
P.O. Box 1490
Sun City, Arizona 85372

Please send _____ copies of **LIFEPLANNING** at $13.95 per book (includes postage and handling).

_____ for 5 to 10 copies send $11.95 per book (includes postage and handling).

_____ Please send volume purchase discount information.

MAKE CHECKS PAYABLE TO LIFEPLANNING

Name_____

Street _____

City _____ State _____ Zip _____

All copies will be sent to the same address unless otherwise specified.

SON

DAUGHTER

NIECE OR NEPHEW

CO-WORKER

FRIEND

OR

SPOUSE

·

BIRTHDAY

GRADUATION

CHRISTMAS

PROMOTION

SHOWER

OR

THANK YOU

LIFEPLANNING MAKES THE PERFECT GIFT!